Testament of Virtue

Testament of Virtue

Living the Lesser-Known Virtues

John H. Timmerman

CASCADE *Books* • Eugene, Oregon

TESTAMENT OF VIRTUE
Living the Lesser-Known Virtues

Cascade Books
An Imprint of Wipf and Stock Publishers
199 W. 8th Ave., Suite 3
Eugene, OR 97401

www.wipfandstock.com

PAPERBACK ISBN: 979-8-3852-4917-6
HARDCOVER ISBN: 979-8-3852-4918-3
EBOOK ISBN: 979-8-3852-4919-0

Cataloguing-in-Publication data:

Names: Timmerman, John H., author.

Title: Testament of virtue : Living the lesser-known virtues / by John H. Timmerman.

Description: Eugene, OR: Cascade Books, 2026 | Includes bibliographical references and index.

Identifiers: ISBN 979-8-3852-4917-6 (paperback) | ISBN 979-8-3852-4918-3 (hardcover) | ISBN 979-8-3852-4919-0 (ebook)

Subjects: LCSH: Character. | Virtue. | Virtues.

Classification: BJ1531 T28 2026 (paperback) | BJ1531 (ebook)

VERSION NUMBER 04/23/26

"The Back Yard," here the conclusion of Chapter Ten, "The Promise of Peace," first appeared in different form in *The Reformed Journal Blog* (9 January 2025).

"What is Grace?" previously appeared in abbreviated form in *Calvin Theological Journal*, 60.1 (April, 2025) 91–103.

FOR PAT

—always the first and best reader

With thanks to Andy Hoffecker,
Pam Hoffecker, and Miriam Lilley
for their careful reading in the early
stages and their helpful suggestions.

Thanks to the Boys: Woody Vanden Bosch,
Tom Swets, John Rozeboom, and Tom
Boersma for lunch hours at the Beltline.

Contents

Introduction

Slaying the Sacred Stone: The Power of Virtue

If one were to venture out into the moonscape wilderness areas of the Middle East, not an advisable thing to do, one would find the hot land littered with stones. These are ancient stones. Archaeology, with its careful brushwork and dating mumbo-jumbo, has dated some of these wind-sanded stones back to three millennia before Christ. Ancient stones, indeed.

It is not surprising that ancient people found these stones in their nomadic wanderings and believed that they were heaved to the surface of the earth by one primal stone at the earth's core. It was the womb, the egg that hatched all living things. Therefore, the stones, and particularly those oblong ones shaped like an egg, were sacred. They signified a birth, our birth. They were fertility and life—emblems of the god of life. And they were lying right there in the dust.

So the people took them, and sometimes carved crude human features on them, and worshiped them as a gateway to the goddess of life. Some large stones were lifted into small temples, facing a perpetual fire. These stones supplied some discretionary privacy for the sacred prostitution that often accompanied them. In that case the sacred stone was accompanied by an exterior Asherah pole, celebrating the goddess of fertility.

For various reasons, the Old Testament Israelites seemed unable to resist the temptations of the sacred stones. To be sure, they had their own stone altars ordained and directed by God. These served two general purposes. First, notable stones were simply used as boundary markers. In Genesis 31 we find Jacob and Laban erecting a "heap" of stones serving as a boundary marker for their properties. Second, a stone or several stones were erected as "a witness" to some spiritual event. In that same chapter of Genesis, the heap of stones "witnessed" that Jacob and Laban parted in peace. This sense of commemoration occurs often in the Old Testament. Exodus 24 records Moses setting up an altar of twelve stone pillars to witness God's revelation in the Ten Commandments to the twelve tribes of Israel. In the ceremony, Moses sprinkled blood of the sacrifice on the pillars.

Other commemorative uses of stones appear in the Old Testament. One of the more carefully detailed accounts occurred when Joshua led the people of God through the Jordan River. When the priests carrying the ark of the covenant entered the river all the rushing water "piled up in a heap" (Josh 3:16) while the people crossed on dry land. After the whole nation crossed, with the priests still standing, Joshua appointed twelve men, one from each tribe, to go back and to select twelve stones from where the priests stood. These stones were to "serve as a sign among you" for when their children would ask "What do these stones mean?" (Josh 4:6). Therefore, "'These stones are to be a memorial to the people of Israel forever'" (Josh 4:7).

Examples could be multiplied. Stones played a vital role in Israelite life and worship. Their God, after all, created heaven and earth and all that is within them, and called them good. The difficulty lay in what significance the individual Israelite attached to the stone. This is a fact that prevails today. One couple, Ron and Ronda, may consider their home a haven for the wayward and weary, a respite where others may come and have their worry and pain alleviated. They invite people over and feed them lavishly. They have a foster child upstairs and one of their own in the basement, still trying to figure out how to flee the nest. Yet their neighbors, Pete and Jenny, may see their home as a barrier against the world. At all costs, and there are plenty, they want to block the world out. Their home is bedecked with cameras, hung with lights, riddled with alarms lest one should try to breach their defenses. They even have an added golden retriever who will roll over and play dead to anyone who will scratch its stomach.

Two houses bear opposing identities because of the people who live there and the purposes they have in mind. It may have been hard at times for a young Israelite male to steer around the sacred stone and the Asherah pole that marked a temple of religious prostitution. And it might be hard for a penniless orphan to resist the few coins they could earn for serving in that temple. About as hard as it is for us contemporaries to resist the many temptations that sneak up on us in everyday living. The nature of sin has not changed much over a few thousand years.

* * * * *

Consider this matter of stones just a bit further, so that we can make some claims for modern Christianity from them. Several times in the Old Testament God had to direct his spiritual leaders to get rid of the sacred stones. For example, in Leviticus 26:1 we find: "'Do not make idols or set up an image or a sacred stone for yourselves, and do not place a carved stone in your land to bow down before it'" (see also Deuteronomy 16:22). King Joram falls squarely into the pantheon of bad kings, but he did one thing good: "[Joram] did evil in the eyes of the Lord, but not as his father and mother had done. He got rid of the sacred stone of Ba'al that his father had made" (2 Kgs 3:2). Again, in 2 Kings we read: "They [Jehu's men] brought the sacred stone out of the temple of Ba'al and burned it. They demolished the sacred stone of Ba'al and tore down the temple of Ba'al, and people have used it for a latrine to this day" (10:26–27). Over and over, the spiritual cleansing slipped back into a dereliction of spiritual order. In 2 Kings 18:4 we read: "He [Hezekiah] removed the high places, smashed the sacred stones and cut down the Asherah poles." It was a nearly constant refrain in Old Testament Scripture as a God-serving king struggled to undo the damage of a king who succumbed to the pressure of the worshippers of Ba'al and other pagan deities.

While the sacred stones were anathema in the Hebrew nation, worse by far was the metaphorical "heart of stone." The Israelites were repeatedly indicted for this hardness of heart, for an insensitivity to the will of God, for individual willfulness instead of worship. Ezekiel prophesies the coming cure to this deathly illness: "They will return to it [land of Israel] and remove all its vile images and detestable idols. I will give them an undivided heart and put a new spirit in them; I will remove from them their heart of stone and give them a heart of flesh. Then they will follow my decrees and be careful to keep my laws. They will be my people, and I will be their God" (Ezek 11:18–20). This would be a coming age, under the reign of the Prince of Peace.

The New Testament holds a magnificent response to the banishment of sacred stones. In this case, Jesus is announced as the one, sure, and sacred stone for the people's worship. Jesus executes a wholesale replacement, not just a breaking down. And what does he replace the sacred stone with? Quoting Psalm 118:22–23, Jesus says: "Have you never read in the Scriptures: 'The stone the builders rejected has become the capstone; the Lord has done this, and it is marvelous in our eyes?' Therefore I tell you that the kingdom of God will be taken away from you and given to a people who will produce its fruit" (Matt 21:42–45). And Peter, here quoting from Isaiah 28:16, writes: "As you come to him, the living Stone—rejected by men but chosen by God and precious to him—you also, like living stones, are being built into a spiritual house to be a holy priesthood, offering spiritual sacrifices acceptable to God through Jesus Christ. For in Scripture, it says: 'See, I lay a stone in Zion, a chosen and precious cornerstone, and the one who trusts in him will never be put to shame'" (1 Pet 2:4–5). In this case, we believers become living stones by being grafted into the sacred stone of Jesus.

In this powerful passage the sacred stones used for evil ends are replaced once and for all by the one living cornerstone. Jesus is the divine antonym to the whispers and lures of darkness. One would think all the noise about the dark world of sacred stones, the smoke-smudged temples, and the sacrifices that coated the stones and floor with blood, were all finished. That is not the state in our modern age. Humanity persists in chasing the lure of darkness as if there were no other alternative. In fact, the broad use of so-called sacred stones is truly astonishing.

Dozens of businesses deal in chakra stones, mostly in lots of seven crystals to align with the presumed seven energy spots in the human body and promote healing. You can purchase a chakra chart for aligning the stones for around twenty dollars. Sacred stone jewelry and collectible minerals sell steadily on many internet sites. Of course, video gamers got in on the game; *Fire Emblem: The Sacred Stones* is a hot seller. Then too, so is Kate Golden's The Sacred Stones Trilogy, described by the publisher, Penguin Books, as "seductive" and "addictive." That's not a warning; it's an invitation. And way back in 2008 the indefatigable Clive Cussler published *The Sacred Stone* to bestseller status. Today stones are hot items, sacred or not, to be worn or written about, rolling or still.

* * * * * *

In 1956 C. S. Lewis published his last, and to his mind his best, work of fiction, *Till We Have Faces*.[1] It is a rich and fascinating work that retells the myth of Psyche. It is the fulfillment, perhaps the *entelechy*, of all his fiction and certainly of all his apologetics. Such themes as the longing for heaven, the perfect sacrifice, the rational Fox versus the romantic Redival, the darkness of paganism and the brightness of heaven, troubled belief and terrified doubt—all these collect in a powerful narrative. Most intriguing, perhaps, is the compelling gravity of the sacred stone in the egg-shaped temple of the pagan goddess Ungit and the full meaning of ancient myths. Lewis held that all myths held a portion of the truth ultimately fulfilled in Christianity. They shadowed ultimate truths. This too shapes the paradoxical tensions of the novel.

The story opens when the Priest comes to the King of Glome to inform him of the need for a ritualistic sacrifice in the temple of Ungit to heal the drought-savaged land. "The victim must be given to the Brute," says the Priest. "The victim is led up the mountain to the Holy Tree, then bound to the Tree and left. Then the Brute comes." He adds that "In the Great Offering, the victim must be perfect" (45). That victim, who turns out to be the King's youngest daughter, Psyche, is the scapegoat. She will bear the sins of the people, so must be sinless herself.

As the sacrificial party advances toward the Holy Tree, Psyche finds herself longing for the mountains. She is eager to go through with the sacrifice, believing that the mystery of Beauty will be revealed to her. As she goes, she passes the house of Ungit, that ancient goddess. Hers is an ugly temple, full of deep shadows and smoke. The "whole thing is a roundish hump, most like a huge slug lying on the field." The narrator (Orual, Psyche's older sister) observes that "This is a holy shape, and the priests say it resembles, or (in a mystery) that it really is, the egg from which the whole world was hatched" (94). The whole temple resembles an oblong, egg-shaped stone.

Much later Orual finds herself seated inside the temple. There before her, in the center of activity, rests the blood-stained "sacred stone which is Ungit herself" (269). As the vigil proceeds, Orual finds herself staring at the stone: "I have said she [Ungit's stone] had no face; but that meant she had a thousand faces. For she was very uneven, lumpy and furrowed, so that, as when we gaze into a fire, you could always see some face or other. She was now more rugged than ever because of all the blood they had poured over in the night. In the little clots and chains of it I made out a face . . ." (270).

1. All quotations from *Till We Have Faces* will be cited parenthetically.

As the novel ends, Psyche is at peace. In a frequent theme of Lewis's, death gave her her true self. Beautiful and selfless in life, she becomes the epitome of those qualities in the next life. Orual has a harder time of it. Believing herself ugly, she feels more allied with the bloody stone and the dark shadows of Ungit's temple. But when the King dies, she rules as the Queen of Glome and serves faithfully and honorably. And in benediction the god tells her: "You also are Psyche." All along, the story has been one of Psyche redeeming Orual.

* * * * * *

In the old dispensation, as T. S. Eliot was wont to say, the righteous kings of the twelve tribes faced a never-ending task of eradicating the sacred stones, the dank temples, and the Asherah poles from the land. It seemed hopeless. These sites usually ranged across mountain or hilltops, some in the stony valleys. As soon as one was destroyed, another popped up in a new spot. They wouldn't even have to dedicate a carved Asherah pole to set up business; they could just build the entrance of the new temple near a tree and call it an Asherah tree. The goddess didn't seem to object too strenuously. And those stones? Remember that the desert was littered with them. The people could always find a new one, pour a little blood on it, and call it sacred. The male and female prostitutes were easily recruited from any city slum. It was a thriving business, dealing in the sacred. In fact, many religious hucksters do it yet today. It was really all so banal, lurking right on the outskirts of daily life. Even when Ba'al was set up next to Asherah, and the market was open for child sacrifice, the protest was minimal.

Over and over again went the tedious slaying of the sacred stones. But nothing really died. The stones live in our hearts, thriving on our life blood.

* * * * * *

Thesis statements, the experts tell me, ought to appear in the first paragraph or two of an essay. I do not think that the reader could be confused by the foregoing evidence. Moreover, years of reading mystery novels have made me appreciate deductive reasoning—tracing the evidence to a conclusion. But I do hope that the reader will embrace the thesis that I have been leading up to: That the sacred stones have not diminished in our time, that they live within us, and that we often turn from the living God to worship the idols we set up in our hearts. As we pursue them, we still pour out our life's blood before them. Those who claim to have no sacred stones clogging their worship life likely have one of the worst: the jagged, gnarly, blood-clotted rock of pride.

The teasing quality of the sacred stones we bow before, worship, and spend our lives pursuing is that they exist within. We don't have to traipse up the mountain to visit the sordid temple. We only have to stop and think. In my youth I overheard my parents or relatives talking about a local bar as a "den of iniquity" or a residence that was "a house of ill repute." Quaint terms for a milder age. But these places still exist behind the closed doors of our hearts. In Psalm 14 David laments: "All have turned aside, they have together become corrupt; there is no one who does good, not even one" (v. 3). Sin is a well-known presence, even though some sinners are quite efficient in covering it up.

In the following chapters I will explore powers that smash these stones that block the spiritual flow of our lives. At life's most fundamental level of living, we face two options. They are as old as Adam, in disguises as new as artificial intelligence. One is to follow the leading of the appetites and achievement of instant gratification. The other road to follow is harder and narrower. It is the pathway of Psyche's suffering, the longing for truth and virtue. This second path replaces the first, replaces it totally.

I write from Michigan, a state of fierce winters that demolish roads. What we discover, those of us who live in Michigan, is that the broken roads cannot be patched. The temporary "hot tar" treatment disappears in the next snow-and-salt "event." Then the hole is only deeper, rougher, sharper. The fanciest of cars falter with blown tires and broken suspensions. No, patches, like one-day vows of rectitude, don't work. The ubiquitous road crews that descend upon the roads each May have to strip all the old pavement up with their monster machines, then lay new concrete or asphalt. And so it goes in Michigan, mile after broken mile.

So too it goes when replacing the vices that so gratify our appetites and promise immediate satisfaction to Psyche's longing. But the vices do not last. Their promised gratification and satisfaction are lies. As we give way to the vices that build up within us like stones, we sink lower under their weight. They have to be rooted out and replaced with virtues. But, I believe that virtues have to be understood in a new way in our new age. Clichés no longer work in a time of hard-edged realities. Just how these virtues work, sanctifying us from within, is the subject of this book.

Chapter One

What Is Grace?

I ASKED AN OLD man.

He had gray hair that the wind tousled. Wrinkles crept into the corners of his face, and age spots dotted the skin. He held a sandwich, overstuffed with lettuce. The edges dripped mayonnaise and brown mustard. He held it in his lap, half-eaten, while he thought. On a round, green table next to him, rested a tall glass of milk and a white china plate holding a half-peeled banana.

We met in his backyard, a land of lush green, umbrellaed by a sky of cerulean. Gardens formed the borders. A birch tree with three trunks stood in the middle of the yard. In its branches songbirds flitted, shuttling back and forth to one of the three feeders in the yard. Each of the feeders, I noticed, was squirrel-proof. Two fat squirrels danced along the fence. They weren't starving.

Then I asked him, "What is grace?"

He looked bemused, staring somewhere out in the distance, maybe at that line where the deepest blue sky met the earth. But that was far past his seeing and was hidden by a million or more trees. A faint smile twitched the edges of his lips. What was left of his sandwich dangled precariously in his hand.

"That's easy," he said. He waited so long to continue that I almost prompted him. "Grace is the goldfinches. In the summer, when their feathers turn bright, they are fat, gold coins falling from the tree. I have counted eight of them on the feeder at one time, so many it looks like a blanket of feathers. That is grace."

Smiling now, he raised the sandwich and took a bite. There was a large mustard stain on his green twill pants.

I thought a long time about what the old man said, and I wasn't satisfied. I searched farther. Until one day I saw her.

* * * * * *

She was twirling on the sidewalk like a ballerina, her arms outflung. She was just a wisp of a girl—I would guess about six years old—clad in white leggings and a sparkling pink dancing dress. The really noticeable thing about her, however, was her shiny, long, light brown hair that reflected the sun into a million scattered diamonds flashing across the sky. As she twirled, the wind blew her hair like a veil across her face. At times all I could see was her smile that stretched joyously, like a tipsy comedian.

From a distance there did not really seem to be anything at all unusual about her. I imagine little girls have danced like that for time out of mind. And I don't know why I had to stop and stare, then draw closer. Except maybe that she smiled at me and seemed to hold out her arms toward me. As I neared, I noticed how very thin her arms were. Purple bruises trailed the length of both arms. The wind blew harder, and the tops of green trees bent toward us. I could hear the rushing of the wind, like ocean waves washing over us.

And then it happened, and I stood frozen, holding my breath.

As she laughed at the sky, a gust of wind, a particularly vicious one, swept over the hedge of arborvitae, lifted the long strands of shining hair from her head, and tore them loose. Like a scuttling animal her wig tumbled in the dirt as I hurried forward to catch it.

She looked stunned, standing still with her arms outstretched. And as I bent for the tumbling hair, I saw how her head was bald and white with blue veins showing. Still, she stood there, arms grown heavy slowly lowering to her sides.

I caught the wig where it landed in a tangled heap against a spirea bush. The bush was blooming with delicate pink flowers. I brushed the dust off the wig, and from the nylon wig cap. She took it from me, adjusted the poly strip, and tightened it over her skull. She grinned enormously, enough for three people, as the light brown strands blew across her face once again.

"That's never happened before," she said.

"It's very pretty."

"Thank you. My kindergarten teacher said she had too much hair, so she cut it all off and gave it to me."

I thought she might know. Even if she was only six. "Tell me," I said, leaning down. "Do you know what grace is?"

"Of course, silly." She raised her hands to shoulder height and held her palms out, as if to say, Anybody knows that!

"Well, what is it?"

"It's the wind." And she twirled so that her tutu made a perfectly straight line and her hair swept like a child's silky blanket over her face.

* * * * *

A wee bit wiser perhaps, certainly somewhat entertained, I decided to work out my own definition of grace, especially what it means to contemporaries, and to begin my further research based on that. But just as I began that ambition, I had this passing thought: Why does one need grace anyway? Does it just float in the air, and you catch it like some pathogen? At the very minimum, logic tells us, grace is given to someone and received by someone. Furthermore, guided by Romans 3:23-24, we see that grace meets a need: "All have sinned and fall short of the glory of God, and are justified freely by his grace through the redemption that came by Christ Jesus." This much all Christian theologies seem to agree on: grace meets the need of sinful humans. I decided to start research on my own.[1]

Research is a tricky rascal. Too narrow and you can't find anything significant. Too big and you feel you're caught in the undertow of waves along Lake Michigan, foundering without a life jacket. Aware of the dangers, I turned to the most logical source: the Bible. Right at the outset, reading into the New Testament, I stumbled over a distinction in John 1:17: "For the law was given through Moses; grace and truth came through Jesus Christ." Well, yes. It was a distinction I would expect. Truly, grace is the theme-word of the New Testament. But what about the Old Testament? One can encounter the word *grace* in dozens of Psalms, also in Isaiah for example, or in Proverbs. Yet few would turn first to the Old Testament— the story, as

1. By this "research" I mean that active reflection that nearly every writer sooner or later resorts to. It means, first of all, talking with others, especially those whose ideas don't comport with your own, prowling through bookstores, or reading a good mystery or biography. We call it "priming the well," the well in this case being the creative mind.

John says, of "the law given through Moses"—to study the theme of grace, even though it teems with shadows and whispers of the New.

Instead, we could call the theme-word of the Old Testament *faithfulness*. If the Hebrew nation would live in faithfulness to this law of Moses, they could be sure that God was faithful to them. A reciprocating action is involved. Therefore, we find in Deuteronomy 7:9: "Know therefore that the Lord your God is God; he is the faithful God, keeping his covenant of love to a thousand generations of those who love him and keep his commands." In David's "Song of Praise" in 2 Samuel 22:26, we find these words: "To the faithful you show yourself faithful." That reciprocating action between two parties seems to be the pattern of the Old Testament, with the exception that God's faithfulness is absolute. As Lamentations 3:21–23 has it: "Yet this I call to mind and therefore I have hope: because of the Lord's great love we are not consumed, for his compassions never fail. They are new every morning; great is your faithfulness."

Emphasizing faithfulness as a primary theme in the Old Testament is certainly not to say that grace is absent. It appears frequently. For example, King Hezekiah sent couriers throughout his kingdom bearing a letter. In the closing lines of that letter, Hezekiah affirms that "The Lord your God is gracious and compassionate. He will not turn his face from you, if you return to him" (2 Chr 30:9). Similarly, in Nehemiah's articulation of the great "Covenant of Love," he remembers God's compassion and fidelity rather than his laws. Even when the Israelites grew rebellious and forgetful of their God, Nehemiah praises God, proclaiming, "in your great mercy you did not put an end to them or abandon them, for you are a gracious and merciful God" (9:31). God's grace is very much alive in the Old Testament; nonetheless, it is true that the accounting of grace is fulfilled in the New Testament because Jesus himself is the incarnation of grace. John announces that "We have seen his glory, the glory of the One and Only, who came from the Father, full of grace and truth" (1:14).

Consequently, the iterations of grace multiply exponentially. Romans, for example, is sometimes called "The Testament of Grace." In Paul's famous comparison of "Death through Adam and Life Through Christ" in Romans 5, he concludes the discourse by asserting that "Where sin increased, grace increased all the more, so that, just as sin reigned in death, so also grace might reign through righteousness to bring eternal life through Jesus Christ our Lord" (vv. 20–21). Furthermore, Paul makes the distinction between the Old Testament dispensation and the New. In Romans 6:14

he adds, "For sin shall not be your master, because you are not under law, but under grace." Perhaps the most succinct and memorable New Testament definition of grace appears in Ephesians 2:8–9: "For it is by grace you have been saved, through faith—and this not from yourselves. It is the gift of God—not by works, so that no one can boast."

Sin constitutes our need; grace is our remediation. That sense of human helplessness called sin is testified to universally. Centuries ago, John Calvin stated that "Man is not possessed of free will for good works, unless he be assisted by grace, and that special grace which is bestowed on the elect alone is regeneration."[2] *The Institutes*, of course, is the handbook for original sin, the one doctrine with more than ample proof. In Calvin's estimation, humans could do no good apart from divine grace: "Whatever good is in the human will, is the work of pure grace . . ."(II.iii.6).

Well before Calvin, however, Thomas Aquinas was working out his notions of sinful humanity and divine grace. For Aquinas "grace" operates at several levels, definitions sliding in and out of each other like ice on a griddle. For example, when humanity was created, grace was imbued in its nature. Grace was the spark of God, the presence of God, or what we might call "the Image of God" in this good thing he had created. When humanity fell into sin, the original sin, this nature was crippled. Now humanity needed some outside presence to supply grace to them. This came in two ways: first, the sacrifice of Jesus, which furnished the grace of eternal life; second, the sacraments to keep humans in a right relationship with God. The sacraments battle the vestiges of original sin—a sin by nature—residual in us.[3]

Contemporary theologians have also put their individual imprint on the varying concepts of grace. J. I. Packer, in his landmark *Knowing God*, argues that "The grace of God is love freely shown towards guilty sinners,

2. Calvin, *Institutes*, II.ii.6. Further quotations will be cited parenthetically.

3. The difficulty in defining grace is not simply spiritual posturing. *The Belgic Confession* calls Jesus's justification of us "this great mystery" (Article 22). And the *Canons of Dort* states: "The manner of this operation [i.e., grace] cannot be fully comprehended by believers in this life. Nevertheless, they are satisfied to know and experience that by this grace of God they are enabled to believe with the heart and to love their Savior" (Article 13). In contemporary studies of grace, one can find nary a whisper about the creeds and catechisms on grace. Yet these church documents are invaluable to understanding both our historical position and also what the Bible has said about grace. Richard D. Phillips is one writer who attempts to rectify this studied ignorance. In his book entitled *What's So Great About the Doctrine of Grace?*, Phillips sets his goal in the Preface: "I aim not merely to teach the doctrines of grace; but to show what is so great about them" (xii).

contrary to their merit and indeed in defiance of their demerit. It is God showing goodness to persons who deserve only severity, and had no reason to expect anything but severity."[4] And Scott Hoezee, in *The Riddle of Grace*, writes: "We could define grace as being first of all that power of God, rooted in his abiding love, by which God forgives the sinful, accepts the unacceptable, revives the spiritually dead, and so enables a reunion between the Creator and his wayward creatures."[5] In Hoezee's estimation, grace calls for a transformation of a way of life to be like Christ. In *Life with God* Richard J. Foster points out that "Christians need grace far more than 'sinners.' In the terrain of life with God, grace is not a ticket to heaven, but the earth under our feet on the road to Christ. . . . Grace saves us from life without God—even more, it empowers us for life with God."[6] Like Scott Hoezee, Foster adds that "Grace is not a system, but a way of life open to all people in the life of Jesus" (190).[7]

Even with a general agreement on the essential meaning of grace, varied emphases provide slightly different slants. For example, in *Mere Morality*, Lewis Smedes observes that "What God expects of ordinary people is obedience born of gratitude; what God gives ordinary people is forgiveness born of grace."[8] Timothy Keller provides a different twist when he writes in *The Reason for God* that "The Christian gospel is that I am so flawed that Jesus had to die for me, yet I am so loved and valued that Jesus was glad to die for me."[9] Part of the varied distinctions inheres in the fact that grace itself has become such a broad and slippery term in modern language. In *What's So Amazing About Grace*, Philip Yancey dances across some cognates of grace: "Many people 'say grace' before meals, acknowledging daily bread as a gift from God. We are grateful for someone's kindness, gratified by good news, congratulated when successful, gracious in hosting friends. When a person's service pleases us, we leave a gratuity. . . . A composer of music may add grace notes to the score. Though not essential to the melody—they are

4. Packer, *Knowing God*, 120.

5. Hoezee, *Riddle of Grace*, 4.

6. Foster, *Life with God*, 179. Further quotations will be cited parenthetically.

7. Foster is insistent that grace affects our actions. In *Streams of Living Water* he writes: "The goal of the Christian life is not simply to get us into heaven, but to get heaven into us" (243).

8. Smedes, *Mere Morality*, 85.

9. Keller, *Reason for God*, 187.

gratuitous—these notes add a flourish whose presence would be missed."[10] I appreciate the way Anne Lamott addresses the ambiguities of grace in *Traveling Mercies*: "I do not at all understand the mystery of grace—only that it meets us where we are but does not leave us where it found us. It can be received gladly or grudgingly, in big gulps or in tiny tastes, like a deer at the salt. I gobbled it, licked it, held it down between my little hooves."[11]

* * * * *

After reading these and other modern authors, I formulated the following definition: Grace is an action whereby one person gives a gift to a person in need who is unable to obtain that gift on his or her own ability. In a specifically Christian understanding, we think of grace as a gift of God to redeem us from our sinful nature, a redemption we can in no way work out on our own. It seems important, moreover, particularly in the light of the forthcoming discussion of Kierkegaard's critique of the present age, to emphasize again that grace is an action on the part of both parties: God and human. It is never a passive thing, or something that happens to us willy-nilly.

Now to the heart of the matter: what about grace today? A few years ago, I submitted to extensive open-heart surgery to correct the destruction that the disease of hypertrophic cardiomyopathy had wrought upon my heart. I had deteriorated over the last few years to a doddering old relic who nearly passed out climbing a flight of stairs or whose blood pressure soared into the stratosphere if I tried to walk around the block. For a period of five hours some machine took over my heartbeat and breathing while the surgeon carved away excess tissue from inside my heart, allowing the blood to flow smoothly once again.

What struck me later about the surgery was its great immediacy. The present moment was never clearer. The surgeon couldn't very well lay down his scalpel and go out for dinner while my heart lay open in need of attention. Even while the machine clicked on and on, serving the body its meal of fresh blood and breath, I was living in the ever-present Now.[12]

10. Yancey, *What's So Amazing About Grace?*, 12.

11. Lamott, *Traveling Mercies*, 143.

12. In his *Grace: More Than We Deserve, Greater Than We Imagine*, Max Lucado creates a not entirely successful metaphor of God as heart surgeon: "Grace is God as heart surgeon, cracking open our chest, removing your heart—poisoned as it is with pride and pain—and replacing it with his own" (10). It may be more reasonable to say that God

The encounter with grace has lost its urgency in the present Now. The very comforts we enjoy induce a vast, spiritual ennui. Back in 1848 Søren Kierkegaard, perhaps the most unpopular man in Denmark, wrote a slim volume titled *The Present Age*. It is a good thing it wasn't longer; its contents are hard to take. Kierkegaard indicts the age as living without passion, without radical commitment to anything. Individuals think about acting upon a principle, but they think so long that the time for action passes by. We get lost, he says, in "reflective tension." Of course, this stasis affects religious affairs: "Equally unthinkable among the young men of today is a truly religious renunciation of the world, adhered to with daily self-denial."[13] We tend to like our worldly ways. We are reluctant to give them up and serve "the Lord your God with all your heart and with all your soul and with all your mind and with all your strength" (Mark 12.30).

A look around us will bear out Kierkegaard's words. Pockets of Christendom still do call for a radical renunciation of the world's ways. Some churches still do practice a living passion for the cross and the Word. Here and there Jesus's sacrifice still does mean something, and believers still think that creeds and catechisms are worth hanging onto. But our look around certainly stumbles over many congregations and denominations that are doing their level best to adapt to culture about us. Tastes and fads and popular thought often drive our theologies. Jesus becomes a hazy historical figure, God Almighty a shuffling saint asleep on his throne, and the Holy Spirit as vaporous as yesterday's mist.

Whatever the case, believers still like grace—especially free grace, but really nothing that will ruffle the even flow of our lives. We live, as Dietrich Bonhoeffer says, in the age of cheap grace: "In such a Church [practicing cheap grace] the world finds a cheap covering for its sins; no contrition is required, still less any real desire to be delivered from sin. Cheap grace therefore amounts to a denial of the living Word of God, in fact, a denial of the Incarnation of the Word of God."[14] Bonhoeffer adds that "Cheap grace is

---

changes, purifies, or redeems our heart, but it is absolutely our own heart we live with, complete with all its fallen temptations and human foolishness. That is why we insist that our need for grace is ongoing. It is the fountain we may keep turning to over and over again. It never runs dry.

13. Kierkegaard, *Present Age*, 36.

14. Bonhoeffer, *Cost of Discipleship*, 44. Future quotations from this edition will be cited parenthetically. Bonhoeffer sounds his battle cry right at the outset of *The Cost of Discipleship*: "In such a Church [practicing cheap grace] the world finds a cheap covering for its sins; no contrition is required, still less any real desire to be delivered from sin.

not the kind of forgiveness of sin which frees us from the toils of sin. Cheap grace is the grace we bestow on ourselves" (44). Furthermore, "Cheap grace is grace without discipleship, grace without the cross, grace without Jesus Christ, living and incarnate"(45). Against this prevailing mood, Bonhoeffer contrasts "costly grace": "Costly grace is the gospel which must be sought again and again, the gift which must be asked for, the door at which a man must knock. Such grace is costly because it calls us to follow, and it is grace because it calls us to follow Jesus Christ. It is costly because it costs a man his life, and it is grace because it gives a man the only true life. It is costly because it condemns sin, and grace because it justifies the sinner" (45). One can tabulate the spiritual health of nearly any congregation by measuring it against those definitions of Bonhoeffer.

Grace arrives through pain. At its center lies an event, not some mysterious and wriggly concept. That event is the cross, and it is memorably offensive. John Stott observes in *The Cross of Christ* that: "[God] pursued us even to the desolate anguish of the cross, where he bore our sin, guilt, judgment and death. It takes a hard and stony heart to remain unmoved by love like that. It is more than love. Its proper name is 'grace', which is love to the undeserving."[15] In his study of the book of Romans, Stott also reminds us that "Fundamental to the gospel of salvation is the truth that the saving initiative from beginning to end belongs to God the Father."[16] The action of grace, because of Jesus's sacrifice on the cross, always initiates with God, but it requires a reciprocating action of acceptance in those gifted by grace.

We can trust God; there is no duplicity in him, or he would be other than God. And we can also trust that his grace is limitless. His grace is abounding. Both the Old and New Testaments speak at length of God's limitless love. But so too is his grace, the expression of his love to us. In Ephesians 3:17–18 Paul emphasizes that Jesus loves without dimension or limit: "I pray that you, being rooted and established in love, may have power . . . to grasp how wide and long and high and deep is the love of Christ." Then Paul goes on to say that Jesus's love is even beyond our capacity to imagine: "Now to him who is able to do immeasurably more than all we ask or imagine, according to his power that is at work within

---

Cheap grace therefore amounts to a denial of the living Word of God, in fact, a denial of the incarnation of the Word of God" (43).

15. Stott, *Cross of Christ*, 83.

16. Stott, *Romans*, 111.

us . . ." (3:20). When Paul talks about Jesus doing "more than all we ask or imagine," he is talking about grace.

Such discussion of the limitless love and grace of God is not confined to the New Testament. Nearly identical metaphorical language of limits occurs in Job 11:7–9. Zophar is speaking, and he asks rhetorically "Can you fathom the mysteries of God? Can you probe the limits of the Almighty?" Then he answers his own questions:

They are higher than the heavens—what can you do?
They are deeper than the depths of the grave—what can you know?
Their measure is longer than the earth and wider than the sea.

God's grace transcends any limits we can impose or imagine. This is a God we can depend on, a God without limits to his grace and love, a God we can trust in all circumstances.

* * * * * *

Finally, it was not so much through research, poring over documents ancient and modern, by which I came to know grace. In fact, I'm not at all sure that one can really know grace that way. I have learned that one can fully know grace only by personal experience.

In 1968 I played the lottery and won the big prize: an all-expense paid tour of South Vietnam. Being big-hearted, I tried to pawn the prize off on someone else. No takers. For some reason they too preferred to remain in graduate school.

Soon after I was running up and down the hills of Kentucky in basic training. From there it was on to "Advanced Individual Training" at Fort Hamilton, in the shadow of the mighty Verrazzano Narrows Bridge in Brooklyn. All of us there knew our next stop would be Vietnam. Everything seemed to have a greater urgency.

It seemed especially daunting to Pat and me, who had only been married for two years at the time and now found ourselves plunged into a life we could never have dreamed. The expectation of 365 days apart felt impossible to endure.

So it was over a few days of leave for Christmas, when I was able to fly home, that Pat and I decided to drive back to New York together. Surely it wouldn't be hard to find someplace for Pat to live, a small, safe, and furnished apartment. And as a nurse, it should be easy for her to find a job in one of New York's many hospitals to pay our way for a couple of months.

That way we would have seven weeks when I could get weekend passes and we could be together. So we believed. So we planned.

We arrived at the outskirts of the city in the dark, stopping at one of those ubiquitous Holiday Inns that stitched the highways together across the US at that time. A clean room and a dinner of red-eye ham—so salty one gulped water for hours after—guaranteed. Nonetheless, we awakened early the next morning. There was an awful lot of New York outside the motel door, and we had given ourselves one day to accomplish this. Then my Christmas leave would be over, and I would have to report back to my base.

We were naively optimistic as we studied the thick Yellow Pages in the motel room and began to make calls to apartment complexes. That was a dead end. We collected several daily newspapers from a newsstand. It was too cold outside to scan them, so we visited a coffeehouse and perused the rental ads. As we started calling, we received the message repeatedly: "It's not furnished. Good luck finding one that is." Or, "I'm sorry, that's been let." But almost always this: "No, we don't rent for two months. Our minimum lease is twelve months."

We decided to drive around the side streets of Brooklyn to see if there were any yard signs or other postings for an apartment. One does not hurry anywhere on New York streets. Fifteen million inhabitants and they're all driving in your lane. We did see one sign, in front of a building so dilapidated that only ghouls and Frankenstein would have rented there. Not my wife. I needed someone who would watch over her. But by now evening shadows were settling in. Our buoyant optimism had long ago deflated. Gray streets seemed like canyons going nowhere. Even our old Buick seemed about to give up.

Weary, and certainly forlorn, we began driving back toward the Holiday Inn. We were taking surface streets back through Brooklyn, roughly paralleling the congested Lower Bay Highway. Stopped at a traffic signal, Pat pointed at a small, brightly lit coffeehouse catty corner from us. "Let's stop there," she said. Later she could not say what made her want to stop there, but we did. We decided to pray and talk about Pat driving back to Michigan tomorrow.

We entered and sat at a small yellow table. Someone had left a newspaper at Pat's place, and she elbowed it aside to make room for her coffee. Mostly we just sat quietly and morosely, semiconsciously measuring minutes and hours until we would have to part. Pat fingered the newspaper, a local Brooklyn paper, actually for the nearby Flatbush area, next to her. The paper was open to the want ads. Suddenly she exclaimed, "Look!" and held the paper out to me. There I read:

One bedroom furnished apartment. Secure home.

Call Grace at ________________.

Of course we called Grace. We went to see the apartment, which was still open. Grace and her husband, Harry, a warm and loving Italian couple, greeted us warmly. We explained our situation: how I would be finishing training, how Pat would be working at a hospital, how we would only be needing the apartment for two months. All of which was fine with Grace, who, we gathered, was the businessperson of the family. We began unloading our paltry belongings from the Buick's trunk.

Grace and Harry helped us as they showed off the ground-level apartment in their brownstone. After welcoming us, Grace turned and said: "I want you both to know that we will be watching over Pat. You have nothing to worry about here."

Nor did we, as we gave ourselves into grace's welcoming hands.

Chapter Two

Mercy

The Forgotten Virtue

Practically anyone can name several of what one author calls "The Glittering Vices."[1] They are showy. They garner lead-off attention on the evening news and the newspapers. We are at once repelled by them and powerfully attracted to them. For the sake of background, the traditional vices are listed in order of Aristotle's original arrangement, from least offensive to the worst: Lust, Gluttony, Greed, Sloth, Wrath, Envy, Pride. Lust is a purely animal instinct while pride is a deliberate act of the will. Before we pursue our search for mercy, a brief mention of the vices would serve us well. As so often happens, we tend to learn about a virtue by examining its negative manifestation as a vice.

Pope Gregory I (540–604) enumerated and codified the vices for the church in the order familiar to us today. In the fourteenth century Dante opened the vices to the literary and philosophical mind in his *Purgatory*. Each of the seven vices, starting with Pride, forms an upper cornice on Mount Purgatory. One must pass through and put off the vice to arrive at Paradise. In her always illuminating Introduction to her translation of *Purgatory*, Dorothy Sayers explains the divine place of the vices: "Only good can originate anything: evil can only deform and corrupt the good

1. See DeYoung, *Glittering Vices*.

already existing."[2] Sayers refers to the vices as "root sins" or the "stain of sin," commenting that "These are the fundamental bad habits of mind recognized and defined by the Church as the well-heads from which all sinful behaviour ultimately springs."[3] When Saint Thomas Aquinas baptized Aristotle by Christianizing much of his thought, these further became known as the "deadly sins" because they can lead to spiritual death. Only confession, repentance, and forgiveness, in Aquinas's thought, can lead us to Jesus's grace that proves the remedy for such sins.

As modern humanity knows all too well, we are an immensely clever people. Our native creativity invents variations on the "Seven Deadlies" all the time. The authors of Scripture were aware of this quality and sometimes expanded the list to fit observable sins. Witness 2 Timothy 3:1–5: "There will be terrible times in the last days. People will be lovers of themselves, lovers of money, boastful, proud, abusive, disobedient to their parents, ungrateful, unholy, without love, unforgiving, slanderous, without self-control, brutal, not lovers of the good, treacherous, rash, conceited, lovers of pleasure rather than lovers of God—having a form of godliness but denying its power." By the time we inspect all the dark splotches on our own souls, we probably stand convicted of nearly all of these and then some.

The vices appear as the root stains of human living. Succubus-like, they move in and inhabit the life and will and thought of the offending human. They eventually become a way of life. So it was that Christianity posited the virtues as a kind of counter-life. Not only do virtues stand over against the vices, but they also form a way of living that invites Christ to be the head and master. In the case of mercy, we also observe a close alliance with three other qualities: generosity, justice, and compassion. Mercy cannot exist without them.

Christianity traditionally arranged its list of virtues into two parts that stand contrary to the vices. The first part is the divine triad that we call the "theological virtues": Faith, Hope, and Love from 1 Corinthians 13. In 1 Thessalonians 1:2–3, Paul returns to these, now showing how the virtues are enacted in life: "We always thank God for all of you, mentioning you in our prayers. We continually remember before our God and Father your work produced by faith, your labor prompted by love, and your endurance inspired by hope in our Lord Jesus Christ." In Paul's relation of the heavenly traits to the physical manifestations of them, each virtue is applied to an action. Faith

2. Sayers, "Introduction," 31.

3. Sayers, "Introduction," 65.

in God undergirds our work; it is cause for it. We labor in a spirit of love, but because of love we labor. Finally, we must endure, but we endure because of hope. In such a light, the virtues are ruthlessly practical.

Historically, Christianity added to the theological virtues these four: prudence, justice, fortitude or courage, and temperance. These are commonly called the "cardinal" virtues, using the Latin word *cardo* for hinge or pivot to indicate their primacy or pivotal importance. They open unto others. Each of them, of course, carries elaborate meanings and definitions, accrued throughout the course of history from Plato to today. For example, today prudence answers to a definition something like "a well-grounded worldview, steady, dependable, marked by a reflective and rational approach." The phrases may be extended nearly exponentially.

The vices have lost a fair degree of attention in this present age. Indeed, with our upside-down moral climate, vices are now often heralded as virtues. Their most useful purpose might be as a tool to point out the foibles and follies of others. The word *vice* itself has lost much of its force. Vice is most frequently understood now as a deviation from the norm. That would be the socially sanctioned norm. As such, vices are not considered intrinsically wrong, but merely as alternative lifestyles. Either that or they are considered the products of a damaged social environment. All this relieves the deviant person or act of culpability.

The virtues, on the other hand, have shown resiliency. Christians have repeatedly used them as thematic study material and certainly as life improvement material. But, as the vices spawned all kinds of subsets of other vices (slander, boastful, abusive, etc.), so too the virtues have biblically and ethically multiplied the original seven. In fact, one might say that the whole New Testament is a primer of how virtues are enacted. Most notably, however, is the way the traditional fruits of the spirit have been used to embellish the virtues: "But the fruit of the Spirit is love, joy, peace, patience, kindness, goodness, faithfulness, gentleness and self-control" (Gal 5:22). Other passages abet this one from Galatians. In Ephesians 5:8–9, we read, "Live as children of light (for the fruit of the light consists in all goodness, righteousness and truth)."

Although the vices have probably been done to death in print, I refer to them here to make the case for virtue, and particularly the nearly forgotten virtue of mercy. While Amazon may offer a dozen or more books on mercy, in habit mercy has fallen out of favor. Most statistical trends suggest that mercy is in its death throes. One habit intimately linked with mercy—a soul sister, so to speak—is generosity. If we understand mercy as giving or kindness to the unwary or undeserving, then generosity seems to be related. John the Apostle frankly questions: “If anyone has material possessions and sees his brother in need but has no pity on him, how can the love of God be in him?” (1 John 3.17).

Very well, one might say, but generosity is not the same as mercy. True. It is a related condition of the soul that generates mercy. Generosity may not be identical to mercy, but mercy requires sacrificial generosity. Here's an example: God so loved the world that he gave his one and only Son that whoever believes in him shall not perish but have everlasting life.

While a spirit of generosity affects the giving of mercy, in the same way justice affects and qualifies mercy. This is not particularly difficult to comprehend. Justice convicts one of something wrong; mercy then meets that need. An example lies in the above quotation from John 3:16. Justice led Jesus to the cross. Humanity's sins had to be paid for in order that humanity might be reconciled to God. This payment was enacted by Jesus on the cross. He alone, being sinless, met the demands of justice, thereby showing mercy to all those who turn to him. Paul puts this nicely in Ephesians 2:4–5: “But because of his great love for us, God, who is rich in mercy, made us alive with Christ even when we were dead in transgressions—it is by grace you have been saved.” The letter to Titus echoes this: “He saved us, not because of righteous things we had done, but because of his mercy” (3:5).

Christianity, therefore, introduces a way of thinking that turns traditional modes of ethical practice on its head. Traditional ethics at the time of Christ, such as it was, saw justice as the deserved punishment for one's wrongdoing. The trick to being just was to levy fair punishment proportionate to the crime. Justice, however, was nearly always abrogated by power, with ethical actions or the lack thereof determined by the person or people in a position of power. Christianity sets a far different course. Lewis Smedes observes in *Mere Morality* that: “At the heart of the gospel, God's kind of justice appears to be a total reversal of ordinary justice. . . . For according to the good news, God does *not* give people what they have coming to them, but what they do not deserve.”[4] Smedes adds that “God had freely given himself in Jesus Christ, who stood in our place as prisoner in the dock and there received the full measure of divine justice. The retributive side of justice was thus settled in Jesus' death (Rom 3:25). The next step was

4. Smedes, *Mere Morality*, 28. Future quotations will be cited parenthetically.

to allow Jesus' righteousness to count as ours" (28). God upholds the virtue of justice; in his mercy God pays the price.

In his teaching, Jesus extends the connection between mercy and justice to showing generosity even to our enemies. In Luke 6:35–36 Jesus is recorded saying: "But love your enemies, do good to them, and lend to them without expecting to get anything back. Then your reward will be great, and you will be sons of the Most High, because he is kind to the ungrateful and wicked. Be merciful, just as your Father is merciful." This is the really radical justice of Jesus: he shows mercy to the undeserving and to his enemies.

We see, then, that the action of mercy, the virtue of mercy, is prompted by two peculiar preconditions of the heart. The first is the generous spirit, so generous that it gives to the undeserving. The second is a heart for justice, but of a most peculiar kind. Jesus's justice turns the standards of this world upside down. Jesus's justice puts himself in place of the guilty one and exonerates the other. It is not unmindful of sin. Indeed, Jesus takes upon himself the full penalty of the sin. But thirdly, we see that divine mercy, our model, is imbued with compassion.

The blessing of compassion composes a powerful biblical theme, extending on an even course through both Testaments. Compassion and mercy meet in several Old Testament books. Already in Deuteronomy the Israelites are warned not to hoard forbidden objects but instead to depend on God: "None of these condemned things [plunder from warfare] shall be found in your hands, so that the Lord will turn from his fierce anger; he will show you mercy, have compassion on you, and increase your numbers, as he promised on oath to your grandfathers . . ." (Deut 13:17). In Nehemiah 9:31 we find a situation where the people had gone astray. Nehemiah says, "But in your great mercy you did not put an end to them or abandon them [the Israelites], for you are a gracious and merciful God." In Psalm 9:13 David pleads, "O Lord, see how my enemies persecute me! Have mercy and lift me up from the gates of death." And Zechariah nicely ties together our allied terms: "Administer true justice; show mercy and compassion to one another" (7:9).

The prophet Hosea speaks at an interesting point in Israelite history. The people went through the motions of their religious customs, but their hearts were not in it. They even offered sacrifices to God, but "They will not find him; he [God] has withdrawn himself from them" (5:6). The people are simply trying to cover up their sins and appease a God with whom they no longer have a vital relationship. In the very next chapter, Hosea delivers the word of the Lord: "For I desire mercy, not sacrifice, and acknowledgment of God rather than burnt offerings" (6:6). In Matthew 12:6–7 we find Jesus speaking these same words: "I tell you that one greater than the temple is here. If you had known what these words mean, 'I desire mercy, not sacrifice,' you would not have condemned the innocent." The next step is to see that extending acts of mercy in fact constitute our sacrifice to God.

The call for mercy appears everywhere in the New Testament. After preaching alongside the Sea of Galilee, Jesus looks out over the multitude and says, "I have compassion for these people; they have already been with me three days and have nothing to eat. I do not want to send them away hungry, or they may collapse on the way." Such examples teach us that Jesus did not just talk a good show about compassion, but he indeed acted upon compassion. One might say he lived it. Paul too sounds the call to compassion. In Romans 9:15–16 Paul quotes Exodus 33:19: "'I will have mercy on whom I have mercy, and I will have compassion on whom I have compassion.' It does not, therefore, depend on man's desire or effort, but on God's mercy." Again, in Ephesians 4:32, Paul entreats his audience to "be kind and compassionate to one another." And Jude even tells us to "Be merciful to those who doubt" (22).

Each of these subsets develop from the writer's practically applied version of them. When we observe that generosity, justice, and compassion are allies of mercy, we are simply saying that there are different practical ways of applying and understanding mercy. In no way have we exhausted these applications in Scripture. James, for example, has a very emphatic take on justice: "Judgment without mercy will be shown to anyone who has not been merciful. Mercy triumphs over judgment!" (Jas 2:13). Jesus himself supplies an interesting twist: ""Woe to you, teachers of the law and Pharisees, you hypocrites! You give a tenth of your spices—mint, dill and cumin. But you have neglected the more important matters of the law—justice, mercy and faithfulness. You should have practiced the latter, without neglecting the former"" (Matt 23:23). In effect Jesus says keep giving what you have been giving but add mercy to it. Mercy is not a substitute for our tithe, for example, but is an attitude of the heart with which we give the tithe.

Jesus's comments in his Beatitudes address (the Sermon on the Mount) further our understanding of the action of mercy. As the "root sins" are the inner birthing ground for a host of other evils, so too we see that mercy is both a condition of the heart and also an action. They live together simultaneously. It is possible, of course, to be extremely generous for essentially selfish reasons: in order to gain the notice of others, or to be recognized as a "good" and generous person. Jesus very directly addresses this sin of vainglory: "Be careful not to do your acts of righteousness before men, to be seen by them. If you do, you will have no reward from your Father in heaven. . . . When you give to the needy, do not let your left hand know what your right hand is doing, so that your giving may be in secret. Then your Father, who sees what is done in secret, will reward you" (Matt 6:1–4).

Jesus does not let the Pharisees off easily in his Beatitudes address. Right after the passage just considered, Jesus turns to their public prayers, flowery and heavily laden, and claims that such receive public attention but no divine attention. Instead of lofty and picturesque rhetoric, Jesus says, "When you pray, do not keep on babbling like pagans, for they think they will be heard because of their many words. Do not be like them, for your Father knows what you need before you ask him" (Matt 6:7–8). Jesus follows with the incomparable simplicity of the Lord's Prayer. If our first understanding of mercy is that it is a condition of the heart, then we observe furthermore that the condition is both deeply private, between the individual and God, and simple rather than complicated in nature.

Additional traits of mercy may surely be mentioned. One exercises mercy, after all, in individual circumstances and often unique ways. Shakespeare, for example, detailed qualities of mercy in the famous scene in *The Merchant of Venice* where Portia tutors the greedy Shylock:

> The quality of mercy is not strained;
> It droppeth as the gentle rain from heaven
> Upon the place beneath. It is twice blest;
> It blesseth him that gives and him that takes. . . .
> It is an attribute to God himself,
> And earthly power doth then show likest God's
> When mercy seasons justice.[5]

Although there are similar references to mercy that we could mention, it would be profitable at this point to open our final concern: What are the use and purpose of mercy today? We recognize that to show mercy to others is a command of God, undiminished in both Testaments of the Bible. We recognize also that it makes pragmatic good sense to exercise a degree of

5. Shakespeare, *Merchant of Venice*, IV.i.182–88.

mercy, guided by generosity, justice, and compassion. By and large, society likes merciful people better than unmerciful. One can nicely advance one's own personal cause by being merciful. If we ignored the mercy marked by generous giving, our churches would soon founder and close, our schools would languish, our programs for the poor and needy, such as the American Red Cross, would wash away with the next flood. There are just all sorts of minor and major needs alike that cry out for mercy.

One could legitimately argue that any social group needs the virtue of mercy to exist and endure as a unified body. Mercy is healing and annealing, the very warmth of love that makes of the many one. Our acts of mercy testify to our love for Jesus; they also show God's love. Moreover, they show the unity in spirit and body of God's people.

That unity, prized in Scripture, is under attack in this present age. The ideal that Jesus spoke of in the Gospel of John has in no way diminished. Jesus said, "Holy Father, protect them by the power of your name—the name you gave me—so that they may be one as we are one" (17:11). He adds, "May they be brought to complete unity to let the world know that you love me and have loved them even as you have loved me" (17: 23). Recognizing the need for unity in mercy and love, because we have received mercy and love, the first issue Saint Paul tackles in First Corinthians is the fractured body of Christ: "I appeal to you, brothers, in the name of our Lord Jesus Christ, that all of you agree with one another so that there may be no divisions among you and that you may be perfectly united in mind and thought" (1 Cor 1:10). Paul stands aghast at hearing of quarrels in the body of Christ. Since believers are united in love with Jesus (Phil 2:1), they ought to be united in love.

A final example bears mention. One of Paul's most moving pastoral letters is that to the Colossians. With piercing clarity and a gentle spirit he tutors the young church in living in Jesus. But, being Paul, he occasionally pauses for a mild admonition: "My purpose is that they may be encouraged in heart and united in love, so that they may have the full riches of complete understanding, in order that they know the mystery of God, namely, Christ . . ."(Col 2:2). That is one of the clearest statements of Paul's goal in his letters: that others may be united in love. And, as we have argued, that union in love is grounded in acts of mercy.

While the unified body of Christ remains the ideal of the church today, one would have to be particularly obtuse to see how woefully contemporary Christians have treated this ideal. Over the past few decades, but increasingly so in recent years, groups of believers in nearly any church have splintered off to satisfy their particular interests or because they have a different interpretation of Scripture. Sometimes they form a new church; sometimes they form a new denomination complete with a seminary. In any event, justice suffers, compassion is turned on its head, generosity of spirit withers, and love for the body of Christ seems forgotten.

As we have seen from the start of this essay, guided by such authorities as Jesus, Paul, James, Matthew, and Moses, that's "not the way it's supposed to be." No one expects all congregants in a church to have an identical mind. That of course threatens the individualism of salvation. There is no corporate salvation, and no salvation by membership in anything. Each person stands individually before God. In an era where congregations of believers seem to fracture with alarming frequency, at a time when feelings grow frayed and worn, when anger and hurt diminish mercy, compassion, justice, and love, it is time to reassess ourselves. Individually. Perhaps we should extend mercy to ourselves, first of all, and then employ it as Christianity's own balm. We need to forgive ourselves even if in our hurt we believe we have nothing to forgive. And then, with sureness of purpose and clarity of mind, we turn once again to Jesus to beg his mercy on us. The challenge to us individually is to live in love and continue acts of mercy. We do so as the body of Christ, Jesus's representatives to a hurting world.

Chapter Three

The Grammar of Love

Like scores of young English PhDs, I spent a good portion of my early career teaching freshman writing courses. It was an interesting experience because I, also like most young English PhDs, had little or no formal training in teaching writing, much less in grammar. At the start, until you build up your course files, you stay about a half-inch ahead of your students. The practical advice you give yourself as a writer, you discover, is the same advice you pass on to your students. This you avoid; this you do.

Writing essays requires a delicate dance of arguing your position, using research sources to support that position, and using your own illustrations. Generally, I don't engage that second step, research, until I have the essay outlined and firmly structured in my own mind. That structure can and often will change as I unearth new things in research. Then the writing goes through many drafts during which things like excessive words, grammar errors, infelicitous style, and flaws in the argument are disabused of their claims to existence.

I mention all this because it has very much to do with this essay on love. I was at that stage where I opened the computer to see whether there were contemporary studies of love that I had to study.[1] The tricky part is

1. Apparently, love is still a hot topic in the publishing marketplace. For example, here are just three of many examples published during the last decade: Jacqueline A. Bussie, *Love Without Limits* (Minneapolis: Broadleaf, 2022), which studies "Polarizing Politics" and other barriers to neighbor love; Paul E. Miller, *Love Walked Among Us*

deciding what to enter into the search engine. So it was that I Googled this: "Contemporary authors on love." What popped up were the author photos of fourteen romance novel writers. Following on the page were several cover photos of romance novels, complete with women in torn bodices and the young men with well-defined musculature who tore those bodices with ease. These were not real people on the covers. Real people get skin cancer, acne pits, and biceps the size of dimes standing on edge. These were cartoons, and so was the "love" the authors wrote about.

Yet, these fictional, cartoon characters are more popular than ever. Romance is now the highest earning fiction genre, grossing a combined total of $1.5 billion a year. Given that the average romance novelist earns about $37,000 per book, that's a whole lot of love being sold. Individually, the books are not all that expensive. One can load up on Amazon for ten to fifteen dollars per paperback. Plus shipping.

I discovered one final thing from my misguided journey into the land of cartoon love: the one requirement of publishers of romances is that the novel has a happy ending. Nothing sad, tragic, or too much like life here. It's troubling as a trend. Maybe every maiden dreams of a shirtless man with a three-day beard sweeping her off her feet. Preferably, he was recently washed and dipped in some pleasing scent. In real life he's probably a social drop-out, smells like a garbage dump, and likes himself a bit more than anyone else. Whatever love is, it takes place in the reality of here and now, in this life of discordant notes.

Love itself should be simple to define. Nearly every source I checked tenders a definition something like "Love is a deep affection for another being." The definition asserts that love is active. It occurs in a relationship sought out and reciprocated. The old myth of Cupid's arrow, striking your heart when your vision falls on a lovely woman, is merely a myth, as escapist as cartoon romance novels. Love, we learn, takes work. For Jesus, it took his life.

If love were only "deep affection," however, we could very well retreat to the land of cartoon romances, kick up our heels, hoist a lemonade, and learn about it in the latest bodice-ripper. In fact, love is a great deal more than deep affection. It is also unwavering commitment. It is Ruth, saying,

---

(Colorado Springs: NavPress, 2014), which studies the way to love as Jesus loves; and Matt Mikalatos and Kathy Kang, *Loving Disagreement: Fighting for Community through the Fruit of the Spirit* (Colorado Springs: NavPress, 2023), which won the 2024 ECPA Book of the Year Award in the category of Faith and Culture. Of course, C. S. Lewis's *The Four Loves* sells steadily year after year, most recently in an edition by HarperOne, 2017.

"Where you go I will go, and where you stay I will stay. Your people will be my people and your God my God. Where you die I will die, and there I will be buried" (Ruth 1:16–17). Love, we learn, "always protects, always trusts, always hopes, always perseveres." It does this even when the dinner is burnt, the fifth tennis match is lost, the eighth Scrabble game in a row ends in a laughable defeat.

To illustrate the flexibility of meanings in *love*, consider one of the foremost statements of God's love, John 3:16. I quote the verse here because, under the pressure of cultural forces, it has been bent to mean things that, grammatically, it is impossible to mean: "For God so loved the world that he gave his one and only Son, that whoever believes in him shall not perish but have eternal life." By focusing upon that first clause, many people today take the text as imprimatur for a universalism of some kind. God loves the world; that settles that. If, in the minds of some, it settles eternal matters, it still has practical implications. For example, if God loves the world, as the independent clause declares, then everyone is of equal worth. The pastor and the prisoner, the prostitute and the parishioner, all stand on equal and complementarian ground. In such a case, then, culture determines orthodoxy, and not the other way around.

But of course, the verse cannot mean that. Wondering just why, I sought out a longtime friend and colleague. In an email conversation, James Vanden Bosch, professor emeritus of linguistics at Calvin University, explained that:

> The adverb clause that comes next provides additional information—sinful humans needed God's son to save them from sin and damnation, and God provided this great gift to a world that needs forgiveness. The final clause . . . includes a noun clause ("whoever believes in him") that functions as the subject of this concluding structure, and its compound verb; this subject-verb unit is an adverb clause describing the consequence of the gift of God's son referred to in the preceding clauses.

That final clause includes a restrictive element; that is to say, "*Only* those who believe in God's son will benefit from this gift."

We moderns tend to talk about love with cheerful indifference toward exactitude. Our daily vocabulary brims over with the word; seldom do we reflect on its full depth and power. High schoolers tend to fall in and out of love on a weekly basis. We love our parents and we love our pet gerbils. We love our friends "to death" as it were, and fall head over heels in love with a new car. In our current times authors have bent their genius to pinning down, defining, praising, and lamenting love. It remains elusive. That fact is particularly regrettable when our land today is scattered widely with those who suffer the pain of lovelessness.

If we spend any time listening to the news, reading a newspaper or news magazines, it appears that today love is in short supply. All around us havoc plays in the streets and homes and especially schools and many begin to suspect that love is not alive and well at all. It is time for redefinition, for setting the course of our love straight. Perhaps we need reminders of first things when they seem to have disappeared into a thick fogbank on the shifting horizon. In this chapter, then, I want to begin with God. It is where any study of love should begin. After noting several traits of God's love, we shift to the nature of human love, and finally to our love for others.

When we are told in 1 John 4:16 that "God is love," brain cells pause for readjustment. Surely God exemplifies perfect love; yes, he sent his son whom he loved to die for us in love; and indeed he teaches us how we are to love. But love itself? That's confounding. Or maybe not, for God is how we know love. His actions toward us define his love. He gave us the supreme example for love in Jesus: "This is love: not that we loved God, but that he loved us and sent his son as an atoning sacrifice for our sins" (1 John 4:10). To look at the necessity for God, we look first to philosophy. To look for the characteristics of God, we look first at how he revealed himself in his book. There we see that God's love is unfailing, saving, and just.

The Israelite nation lived in spiritual uncertainty. Neighboring tribes were polytheistic, with different gods reigning for varied lengths of time throughout the year. The people followed a calendar of religious feasts and pagan festivals to get the right deity on the throne at the right time. It was important, for example, to get Ba'al, the fertility god of the earth, on the throne during planting season. Since Ba'al was also the god of rain and dew, it was best to keep him there during the growing season. Thus, the Canaanite people practiced sacrifices to Ba'al, including child sacrifice, at key times of the year. These would induce Ba'al to rise and rule. Once the harvest was in, a god of sterility and drought could arise and assume the throne. Ba'al would take a seasonal nap. When the time came, blood would again be shed to speed his passage to the throne.

One can imagine the spiritual chaos associated with the different gods for different seasons and events. It is a wonder that the Israelites were attracted to this mess of pottage, but they were—over and over again. One can only explain this psychologically. The idols of all the polytheistic tribes gave a god one could see. You could pull this deity out and prop him on the dresser anytime you wanted. Then dump him back in his travel bag.

Unlike all the polytheistic gods, the Lord Jehovah identifies himself first and foremost as "one God." He stands apart from all the dying and rising gods. God is absolute. There is none other beside him, no one to take his place on the throne. God needs no other referent than himself. He is still the Lord of the burning bush, the "I Am That I Am." He is Creator God and Everlasting God. He loves because he is love. Unlike the polytheistic gods, whose statues still exist in some museums, no one has ever seen God. What we see are the effects of his love: miracles then and miracles now. We see lives changed from despair to delight, from dissipation to devotion.

The nature of God's eternal love is characterized by other traits. For example, God's love is unfailing, as Psalm 6:4 testifies: "Turn, O Lord, and deliver me; save me because of your unfailing love." God's love, furthermore, provides protection: "Because of the Lord's great love we are not consumed" (Lam 3:22). Out of love for us, God adopts us into his eternal family: "How great is the love the Father has lavished on us, that we should be called children of God! And that is what we are!" (1 John 3:1). And how does that adoption occur? God turns the tables on all the polytheistic religions. He spilled his blood that we might rise. First John 4:10 has it: "This is love: not that we loved God, but that he loved us and sent his son as an atoning sacrifice for our sins."

A list of traits of God's love could be extended; everywhere the Psalms exalt God's love that endures forever. But in the very midst of such a love fest, the Bible, which if anything is a document in realism, throws discordant notes. Even in the exquisite phrases of 1 John, the disquieting words arise: "Do not love the world or anything in the world. If anyone loves the world, the love of the Father is not in him" (1 John 2:15). It is there in the Old Testament too: "For I, the Lord, love justice; I hate robbery and iniquity" (Isa 61:8). Or, "I hate and abhor falsehood" (Ps 119:163). How can Love hate?

In his landmark study of Christian ethics, *Ethical Reflections*, Henry Stob includes an addendum in which he wonders if a God of love, who *is* love, can hate. To be sure, we see many instances of God's wrath in Scripture. An example occurs in response to Hezekiah's prayer for deliverance when surrounded by Sennacherib's army. In response, God sent one angel who during the night killed 185,000 Assyrian soldiers (2 Kgs 19:35–36).

That's like destroying a fair-sized city. It also constitutes a fair-sized act of wrath.

The picture we get of God in the Old Testament is that he is a faithful God, compassionate and loving: "The Lord your God is gracious and compassionate. He will not turn his face from you if you return to him" (2 Chr 29:9). However, when his compassion is scorned, his wrath arises. In 2 Chronicles 36 we have the sad record of evil kings and the decline of the chosen people into their chosen sins. Consequently, "The Lord, the God of their fathers, sent word to them through his messengers again and again, because he had pity on his people" (36:15). But what was the effect? "They mocked God's messengers, despised his words and scoffed at his prophets until the wrath of the Lord was aroused against his people and there was no remedy" (36:16). In this case, God removed his protective power, allowing Nebuchadnezzar to defeat them and carry them off to Babylon.

With a reckless naivete, some critics of Christianity suggest that the Old Testament is a record of God's wrath and the New Testament is a record of God's love. The cure lies in reading both testaments. The dominant theme of the Old Testament is, as we have seen, the faithfulness of God. Truly, the New Testament's dominant theme is God's love through Jesus, but this in no way obviates or even obscures God's capacity for wrath against sin and evil. In *Ethical Reflections*, Stob asserts: "Can this disposition—which we call hate—in any sense be attributed to God? Yes, in one sense it can. God wants to destroy . . . negate, banish, and reduce to non-existence pride, injustice, cruelty, lying, in short, all wickedness and vice, all sin and evil. These things he hates with a native, essential, and everlasting hatred. He is against them absolutely."[2]

That God hates and will punish sin and evil, then, does not seem open to question. That God permits sinners to suffer the due consequences of their sin seems abundantly manifest in Scripture. But does God hate certain humans? Stob thinks not: "God hates no man! It is Satan and the demons who hate men. . . . Hate of men is against the very law of love, hate of men is the very antithesis of the divine." He adds that "Hate of evil is a divine necessity; hate of men is a divine impossibility" (254).

We might ask, what of hell, then? Doesn't hell contain the very worst sorts of sinners? But we are reminded that hell is not a matter of love or hate; it is a matter of justice. Hell is the province of sinners who have not sought God's loving forgiveness. It is a matter of people who have willfully

2. Stob, *Ethical Reflections*, 253. Future quotations will be cited parenthetically.

turned their backs on God, and who now have God turn his back on them for all eternity. Hell is earned.

In C. S. Lewis's novel *The Great Divorce*, a busload of travelers from Greasy Town, a suburb of hell, arrives at the crisp, solid outskirts of heaven. There they meet heavenly representatives called Bright Spirits, who explore the condition of the ghastly travelers and who reveal glimpses of the Deep Heaven that lies further on. The travelers are marked by two things in particular: their insubstantiality and their persistent demand for personal rights. They just cannot let their old selves go. Thus, no further movement into heaven can be made. The Bright Spirits, on the other hand, represent light and love, a sense of living for something or someone larger than themselves.

In a sense we are very much like the Bright Spirits situated on the fringes of heaven. We are certainly "in love"; that is, in God's love. Furthermore, we are in the kingdom of heaven, even if not yet fully. In fact, most of us still have one foot in Greasy Town and cannot shake it loose. Living in love entails certain obligations and qualities. Lewis Smedes observes in *Mere Morality* that "Love is a command as truly as it is a gift, a duty as much as a power" (45). Before we celebrate our freedom in love, then, perhaps we should examine those duties and obligations upon us.

First among these is the recognition that the Lord who loves us is also the Lord of the universe. In Philippians 2 Paul simultaneously praises the humility of Jesus and the Lordship of Jesus. He leaves us the memorable verses:

> God exalted him to the highest place
> and gave him the name that is above every name,
> that at the name of Jesus every knee should bow,
> in heaven and on earth and under the earth,
> and every tongue confess that Jesus Christ is Lord.
> (Phil 2:9–11)

This is not the loutish hero of some romance novel. This is the Lord before whom the demons tremble (Jas 2:19).

Furthermore, we find nothing soft and fuzzy about Jesus's death. Even in his risen body, Jesus bears holes in his hands, a wound in his side, and scars on his forehead from when he shed his blood in love for us. God's love hurts; it hurt the Trinity—surely God and the Holy Spirit suffered in

Jesus—and it killed Jesus. In all our lovely ballads of God's tender comfort, we remember what it cost God to give it.

Understandably, then, we discover that God's love places certain obligations upon our love. First, when living in love there are certain things to be avoided. In Isaiah 61:8 the prophet speaks God's will: "I, the Lord, love justice; I hate robbery and iniquity." Related instructions thread through Scripture. Fair scales are demanded for weighing. Cheating and hedging are not compatible with love. Several times in Scripture obedience is associated with loving God. For example, John 14:15 states: "If you love me, you will obey what I command." And in the very next chapter we find, "If you obey my commands, you will remain in my love" (15:10).

Live honestly, live obediently, but most importantly live humbly. Most are familiar with Micah's injunction, "What does the Lord require of you? To act justly and to love mercy and to walk humbly with your God" (6:8). Humility is a regular theme in the New Testament also, evidenced most explicitly in Jesus's life and teachings. Humility as a way of life stands over against the most primal sin and the direst threat to love: pride. Romans 12:16 puts it thus: "Live in harmony with one another. Do not be proud, but be willing to associate with people of low position. Do not be conceited." Pride always separates. It elevates self at the expense of the other. It is widely held in the Judeo-Christian tradition that the first sin occurred in heaven, when Satan's overweening pride led him to seek God's position itself. Jesus says, "I saw Satan fall like lightning from heaven" (Luke 10:18). Regarding the first sin on earth, Saint Augustine argued that it too was pride, for surely Adam and Eve set their desire higher than God's command before they ever touched the fruit. In *City of God* Augustine argues: "The point here is that the first man had been so constituted that if, as a good man, he had relied on the help of God, he could have overcome the bad angel, whereas he was bound to be overcome if he proudly relied on his own will in preference to this wisdom of his maker and helper, God."[3] Turning from God to self-will is the fundamental action of pride; the results are always destructive.

Pride is a cancer in the soul of love. It devours all things, including people, to satisfy its perverted cravings. Pride is to love what darkness is to light. Pride's adamant self-sufficiency gives it warrant to use things and people as it wishes for its own gain. Especially, pride cannibalizes justice.

3. Augustine, *City of God*, XIV.27, 320. And also, "Our first parents, then, must have fallen before they could do the evil deed, before they could commit the sin of eating the forbidden fruit" (XIV.13, 309).Future quotations will be cited parenthetically.

If God's requirements to exist in his love include honesty and obedience, the requirement to live in justice provides the unified life plan for both of them. Justice is at the heart of Christian love and is the opposite of pride. Pride subsumes all things into a vortex of self-gratification; justice works outward, living to help others.

Pride, it seems to me, lies at direct odds with both justice and love. Worse, it impedes and harms the course of justice. Our culture is infected with the virus of wanting "to get ahead." Often this means the accumulation of goods and precious objects at the expense of time with family, friends, and Jesus. Moreover, pride lords it over others and often behaves toward others superciliously, biting and mean. Pride beholds others as "less than . . ." Pride just does not much care about other things or people. Then, of course, one does not have to read far in Scripture to see that God hates pride. C. S. Lewis observes in *Mere Christianity* that proud people are so busy looking down on others, that they fail to look up toward the one Person who is eternally higher.[4] Pride ignores God, at its peril. Isaiah 13:11 says that God "will humble the pride of the ruthless."

If one loves truly, one will seek redress or justice for the lives that pride has ruined. While pride is the opposite action from love, justice is the necessary companion. If we pretend at all to anything like Christian love, or love for Christ, we are obligated to act as his disciples in a lonely and wounded world. Examples abound in Scripture. In Job's defense of his life, he leans on his loving deeds for others: "Whoever heard me spoke well of me, and those who saw me commended me, because I rescued the poor who cried for help, and the fatherless who had none to assist him. The man who was dying blessed me; I made the widow's heart sing" (Job 29:11–13). In 1 John 3:17–18 the same note is struck: "If anyone has material possessions and sees his brother in need but has no pity on him, how can the love of God be in him? Dear children, let us not love with words or tongue but with actions and in truth."

Someone might object that "having pity" on your neighbor is not the same as loving them. And merely to help someone in need is not necessarily justice. We have to pause and ask, "What is justice?" Philosophers of ethics will answer that justice recognizes that people have individual rights, including the right to exist, to have shelter and food. If we go further back to Plato, we would turn to *The Republic* and answer that the just society is the ordered society. This would be the society where each person operates

4. Lewis, *Mere Christianity*, 111.

in his or her own sphere or calling without intruding on that of a neighbor. If we live in the society called Christendom, we might turn to Isaiah 61:2–3 and answer that what the Lord wants for us is "to comfort all who mourn, and provide for those who grieve in Zion—to bestow on them a crown of beauty instead of ashes, the oil of gladness instead of mourning."[5] Or perhaps Proverbs 14:31, "He who oppresses the poor shows contempt for their Maker, but whoever is kind to the needy honors God." It is this sense of love as an active, dynamic power that led Lewis Smedes to claim: "Love is a power that rises from our soul's need. It is also a strength that flows from our soul's fullness. It drives me to seek another for my sake; it moves me to help another for his or her sake. Love seeks and love gives."[6] Justice recognizes that *love* is an action verb; the required direct object is everyone with whom we come in contact. Beyond the rules of grammar, however, in the alchemy of God's unfathomable, miraculous, and immutable love, even fitted into our fallible minds and hands, we become one with that person we serve in love.

The sad truth of modern culture is that there are many, too many, persons uncertain whether anyone loves them. Innumerable cringing and bruised spirits feel only hate and hurt. We read of horrors happening in people's bedrooms and in nurseries. We live in a land of unmitigated darkness of the soul. Yesterday's shame is today glorified in parades and banners. Base animal instincts rule our higher selves. Pride lives in a house large enough to house a hundred homeless. Twenty miles from where I sit billionaires from Michigan, Indiana, and Illinois have built opulent mansions on the shores of Lake Michigan. Their pools, helicopter landing pads, and cavernous rooms sprawl over the sand dunes and down to the beach. One mogul purchased a string of neighboring cottages. He built elaborately elevated and enclosed walkways between them so he won't get sand in his shoes. It all sounds like nothing quite so much as Milton's Satan, who snarls, "Better to reign in hell than serve in heav'n."[7]

Pride is not only the first sin, standing like a dam in the flow of love, but it is also the most enduring sin. The human story of pride stretches from our first parents to our present moment. Yet, there is one towering

5. Although there are several historical studies of Christianity and justice, the seminal works in contemporary philosophy are three by Nicolas Wolterstorff. These include *Until Justice and Peace Embrace*; *Justice: Rights and Wrongs*; and *Justice in Love*.

6. *Mere Morality*, 45.

7. *Paradise Lost*, 1.263.

story of pride that merits attention here. It has to do with the Israelites and their longing for a king.

It's easy to get exasperated by the Israelite nation in the Old Testament. As a people they were often simply disgusting. God's chosen people had little nobility about them. Nearly every page of their history holds an accounting of some new sin or deviation. While God is revealing himself as their Lord and listing commandments for a right relationship, the Israelites bow before idols. They wanted nothing quite so much as to be like other nations. They craved wealth. They pursued possessions. They rejoiced in plunder. They were so stubborn that God himself called them stiff-necked, a word for pride. Their arrogance reached an apex when they appeared before Samuel to demand a king: "The people refused to listen to Samuel. 'No!' they said. 'We want a king over us. Then we will be like all the other nations, with a king to lead us and to go out before us and fight our battles'" (1 Sam 8:19–20). Like a father giving in to a teenager's pleadings, God simply turns the Israelites over to their own devices. He tells Samuel to give them a king.

Saul, the chosen one, seems at first all things wonderful to all people. Tall, handsome, and a warrior of the first order, he makes the Israelites' hearts sing. When Samuel anoints Saul, the Holy Spirit descends upon him in a powerful way. Samuel says, "The Spirit of the Lord will come upon you in power, and you will prophesy with them [the prophets of Gibeah]; and you will be changed into a different person. Once these signs are fulfilled, do whatever your hand finds to do, for God is with you" (1 Sam 10:6–7). Now this is a king better than all the other kings, full of the spirit of God!

The Israelites began to grumble a bit when Saul drafted their sons into his army ("whenever Saul saw a mighty or brave man, he took him into his service"). When he annexed their property and permanently borrowed their servants, their anger darkened. Although Saul had a way with war, he tended to play God in his own little world: "Saul has gone to Carmel. There he has set up a monument in his own honor" (1 Sam 15:12). Saul worshipped Saul. Samuel rebuked him often, then finally withdrew in silence. Whereas Saul was once full of the Spirit of God, "Now the Spirit of the Lord had departed from Saul, and an evil spirit from the Lord tormented him" (1 Sam 16:14). Saul was so full of himself there was no room left for God, nor for justice and love.

It is a story to make one weep. Blessed with so much, how can one lose it all through stubborn pride? Yet it is a story, albeit with differing plot lines, we see repeated every day. It is time to revise the narrative. Believers are called by their Master to live in unity and love, not in niggling differentiation. Do we worship for our own sake, or the sake of the one Lord who calls us to worship? The answer has never been in question. Our willingness to give up our pride, and to live in loving unity is.

Chapter Four

Be Strong in the Lord

The Mystery of Meekness

One of the salient verses of the Old Testament appears in Deuteronomy 31:6: "Be strong and courageous. Do not be afraid or terrified of them, for the Lord your God goes with you." The encouragement to be strong and courageous is repeated to Joshua twice more in Deuteronomy, five more times in the book of Joshua, and it appears twice in 1 Chronicles. The reason for the encouragement historically was simply the fact that the Israelites would encounter powerful enemies in the promised land that they would have to subdue. The psychological and spiritual reasons, however, are spelled out in Deuteronomy 31:8: "The Lord himself goes before you and will be with you; he will never leave you nor forsake you. Do not be afraid; do not be discouraged." One is always strong in the presence of God.

This concept of our strength originating in the Lord is profound in the Old Testament, referred to multiple times. For example, in Nehemiah 8:10 we find that "The joy of the Lord is your strength." In Psalm 28:7 David declares: "The Lord is my strength and my shield; my heart trusts in him, and I am helped." Repeatedly the prophets turn to God to renew their strength. In the always moving words of Habakkuk, the prophet finds the fruit trees withered, the sheep pens empty, the cattle stalls vacant. Yet he declares that "I will rejoice in the Lord, I will be joyful in God my Savior. The Sovereign Lord is my strength" (3:18–19). One could imagine the prophet standing in war-torn Kyiv or in Gaza or indeed in the hurricane-blasted shambles of Florida or North Carolina and murmuring the same words.

When one reflects on strength, both one's individual strength and also one's dependence upon another for strength, it begins to make one wonder just what kind of a Christian Jesus wants one to be. Paul nicely says, "When I am weak, then I am strong" (2 Cor 12:10). We live well removed from St. Paul's Heraclitean-like paradox. We tend to measure individual strength by the number of reps we can do at the local health club. Truly strong people run great distances, perform in professional sports, and make the rest of us feel foolish. Especially, as is my case, if you're disabled. Then I am told to be strong in the Lord. But I'm told further to be strong by being meek, that meekness in fact is a virtue. That apparent paradox is what I would like to explore with you in this chapter.

Strength in the physical sense is a good thing. By and large we prefer it to being weak. But physical strength as such registers little notice in the Bible, and that often in a negative sense. A super-sized pagan known as Goliath was physically strong, but we remember him largely for his earth-quaking faceplant. That and his very large head rolling across the turf while David leaned on the sword. Repeatedly the Israelites invoked God's help against strong enemies. The adjective sometimes referred to physical size, as in the people of Goliath's hometown, the city of Gath. The 2019 archaeological expedition at Gath uncovered buildings and features of preternatural size, nicely fitting a population of giants. (Further biblical accounts of frightening giants appear in Genesis 6:9; Numbers 13:32-33; Ezekiel 32:27; 2 Samuel 21; and 2 Chronicles 20:4–8.) It is sufficient to say that physical size struck fear in the Israelites repeatedly.

One example of the people's fear before larger forces will suffice. In 2 Chronicles 20 we have recorded the campaign of King Jehoshaphat against Moab and Ammon. Actually, it was a campaign to survive as a kingdom since the invading armies were huge, overwhelming Judah. The first step Jehoshaphat takes is to bow in prayer: "O Lord, God of our fathers, are you not the God who is in heaven? You rule over all the kingdoms of the nations" (20:6). Then the prophet Jahaziel gave the Lord's answer: "Do not be afraid; do not be discouraged. Go out to face them tomorrow, and the Lord will be with you" (20:17). The familiar pattern in Scripture, then, is that the strength of God's chosen people lay in God alone. As long as the leader and the people trusted in God, no physically strong foe could stand against them.

Consequently, the great danger for God's people consisted in the belief that they were strong in their own physical strength, apart from the Lord. Examples are too numerous to list, but one glaring case might show the pattern. When Rehoboam achieved power in Judah, his first task was to build up his 180,000-man army to assure his power and to solidify the Hebrew nation by conquering Israel. When God's prophet talked him out of that venture, Rehoboam set about fortifying all the cities in Judah militarily. His thinking must have gone something like, "If I can't attack Israel, I'll make sure they can't attack me."

Rehoboam's kingdom became bloated with strength. For him *strength* equaled power and self-sufficiency. It even appeared in his family size, with his eighteen wives and sixty concubines, twenty-eight sons and sixty daughters. Rehoboam was a dynasty unto himself. The result seems inevitable: "After Rehoboam's position as king was established and he had become strong, he and all Israel with him abandoned the law of the Lord" (2 Chr 12:1). In the end Rehoboam "humbled" himself before the Lord and thus escaped total destruction. It was up to his son Abijah to defeat Israel militarily, because, as Chronicles reports, "They relied on the Lord, the God of their fathers" (2 Chr 13:18).

Here is what we discover, then, about strength as it develops in the Old Testament. The Israelites were at varied times both deathly afraid of the apparent strength of their enemies, and also very proud of their own strength as measured in military might and possessions. In the same way, when faced with strong enemies they called on God for help; when luxuriating in their possessions they conveniently forgot about God. No one that I'm aware of has ever called the Israelites "steadfast." They pretty much followed wherever the winds of the spirit and circumstance blew.

But to survey briefly the Israelites' mistaken notions about strength and self-sufficiency, to deduce from the evidence that they were guilty of the sin of pride, and to gently condemn their overweening militarism, is still to miss the point. Throughout, the Bible provides us story examples from which we conclude the lessons. It doesn't deal much in aphorisms or maxims as is the fashion of Confucius's *Analects*. It actually doesn't do much in the way of setting rules as is the fashion of Mohammad's Qur'an. The primary narrative fashion of the Bible is a dramatic historical story along with some searching letters. From these we may interpret lessons or concepts that affect our living. Indeed, there may be much controversy over just what is the proper lesson or concept. But that only speaks to its enduring richness and complexity as a piece of God-spoken literature. The Bible is anything but static. I mention this because 1) the Bible has much to say about strength and pride throughout its pages, and 2) this very breathing vitality of Scripture predisposes it to all kinds of wrongheaded ideas and lessons. It has been said of proof texting that any idea whatsoever can be supported by Scripture. For that reason, we have to tread carefully.

The further reason for my caution is that our present age is rife with warring Christian factions, all of whom claim the final, infallible word and all of whom claim to be supported by Scripture. There are also those who claim that certain passages were only relevant to the first-century church, and they do not apply to our more informed age. A text such as Romans 16: 17–18 rightfully gives us pause: "I urge you, brothers, to watch out for those who cause divisions and put obstacles in your way that are contrary to the teaching you have learned. Keep away from them. For such people are not serving our Lord Christ, but their own appetites. By smooth talk and flattery, they deceive the minds of naive people." Paul has similar words in 1 Corinthians 1:10: "I appeal to you, brothers in the name of our Lord Jesus Christ, that all of you agree with one another so that there may be no divisions among you and that you may be perfect in mind and thought." However forcefully biblical writers speak out against division and splits in the church, our age continues to spawn them with abandon. We invent the "cause of the month" and establish a new church to validate it. Like a fibula broken several times, the limb does not grow stronger but weaker. The fractured modern church is in desperate need of mending in the strength of unity.

Perhaps we may agree first that no one cares to be weak. We can also agree that *weak*, like *strong*, has multiple meanings. Allow me a personal example. For a few years in the dusty past, I managed a men's softball team comprised mainly of the halt, the lame, and the nearly blind. We answered to many adjectives, but *strong* was not one of them. We sported gray hair, large waistlines, and weak limbs. The oldest among us was in his eighties. He wasn't very good either. His virtue was that he hit the ball toward third base so slowly that he could rather leisurely hobble to first base and be safe. Once there he asked for a runner, a designated speedster in his mere sixties. Nonetheless—well, largely through the ineptitude of other teams—one year we won the league championship. If others laughed at our softball wizardry, God smiled upon us.

Now, slow-pitch softball is not terribly taxing, designed as it is for old men who don't have better sense. The pitches loft heavenward and descend at a glacial pace. If the ball falls anywhere in the vicinity of home plate, you're encouraged to swing at it. Only once per pitch. Although there are rules against it, most of the bats are highly illegal engineering marvels. If you manage to touch the ball or even get near it, you have a pop fly that lands with a Herculean thud just past the second baseman's outstretched glove. Obviously, it is now the outfielder's ball, so the second baseman watches while two or three others rush to the ball. By now the base walker—we did away with runners—is storming toward second. One outfielder bobbles the ball, another finally throws it in the general direction of first base. The base walker, shedding sweat and pounds, lumbers into third. The first baseman drops the throw. Gasping for breath, the base walker now staggers across home plate. He's quickly tended to with offers of water and a seat on the bleachers. Another in-the-park home run. There is little room for individual pride in this foolishness. Just some kind of joint pride in having prevailed together against all obstacles large and small. We have a party at someone's swimming pool and relish our grand accomplishment. For a whole year we will be champions. Though we are weak we are strong.

It is a whole lot like Christianity. Some singularly puzzling verses in Scripture occur in that first chapter of 1 Corinthians. So fundamental are they to understanding Christianity that I quote the passage at length:

> Brothers, think of what you were when you were called, not many of you were wise by human standards; not many were influential; not many were of noble birth. But God chose the foolish things of the world to shame the wise; God chose the weak things of the world to shame the strong. He chose the lowly things of this world and the despised things—and the things that are not—to nullify the things that are, so that no one may boast before him. (1 Cor 1:26–27)

In other words, Jesus chose people like my softball team, and elevated those poor, frail people to champions.

The really odd thing about Christianity is its tendency toward reversal of expectations. In a way, it's a bit like Aristotle's old term from *The Art of Poetry* called *peripety*, or a sudden change in circumstances. Christianity works so often wholly against cultural expectations. Let me give an example.

Our contemporary culture prizes nothing quite so much as being known. The other day I checked some Christian publishers online for a book I am writing. Several publishers stipulated that they would only consider books from authors who already had over 20,000 followers on a blog or podcast. I can see the point of this. Publication and marketing can be an expensive business, and it's good to have a built-in audience. Still, I wondered. What about the writer that just spends her time writing, working ceaselessly at the craft that she hopes encapsulates the truth and leads others to it? Although an avid reader herself, and a strong supporter of the local independent bookseller, she has never in her life spent her time reading someone's blog. And she has no more know-how to create one than she does for building a computer. Yet increasingly Christian publishers in particular have come to expect this, along with a healthy list of publications. Some even expect the writer to foot part of the bill for publication or typesetting. I suppose the writer pays for this through all the books she isn't selling.

Some time ago my daughter, and she should know better, asked me how many friends I had on Facebook. Since she set up the account for me many years ago already, I suppose she had a right to know. Still, I had to think a moment before I responded, "I believe I have four. Maybe six." Actually, I feel as if I have plenty of friends, more than enough. To me a friendship is a relationship that has stood the test of time. You and your friend have shared not only great happiness, but you have also endured times of grinding sorrow. You generally do this in person. However, when I told my daughter the truth of the matter, that I probably had fewer than a half-dozen Facebook friends, she groaned dramatically and led me to understand that many people had hundreds, some thousands of Facebook friends. I stared at her in disbelief and said that I didn't even know a hundred people.

Underlying the craze for numbers is the belief that being known by many people somehow affirms the reality of your own existence. Numbers confer Being. But Being, at least one's own reality, apparently increases and diminishes in importance according to your online followers. Just what are they following? The projection you make of yourself, not your true self. If you are a sufficiently good raconteur, an accomplished liar, or successful narrator of fictions, you will officially (numbers don't lie!) satisfy yourself that your Being has validity.

God cares very little for your Facebook fabrications, even less so for your patent falsehoods. What God cares about, unbelievably, is you. The tricky thing here is that since the dawn of time God has known you, and he wants the *you* he created back. He wants you to live with him forever, not just a day on Facebook. And since he designed you, handcrafted you one might say, he knows every wart and wrinkle on your true Being. He knows every falsehood you have spun, every fictive house you hide in. And yet, and this is really unbelievable but nonetheless true, he still loves you like crazy. So much so that he will give back to you your real, forever Being. The one you have been longing for in every story you've ever told.

So, the first thing we learn, and it should come as no great surprise, is that God deals in Truth. And after God and you have met and talked over the Truth of the real you, God will do this most unlikely thing: he will give to you the True self you have been longing for all your life. But there is a second way in which Christianity subverts cultural expectations. That has to do with strength.

The danger of strength, as we observe it both in the Bible and in life, is that it evokes a spirit of self-sufficiency and arrogance. Both of these qualities are subsets or characteristics of pride. If we break it down biblically, we would conclude that the bad use of strength is power, and the powerful are often proud and arrogant. Scripture inveighs against this state for the simple reason that such power is forever taking; its greed is never assuaged. Power is a vacuum, inhaling people and things to sustain itself. As such it stands at odds with Christianity, which *de facto* is a giving religion. The central event is that Jesus gave his life for us, a patent absurdity by any other religion. And power, always intent first of all on sustaining itself and growing in power, shakes its head in dismay. In Proverbs 8:13 Wisdom says, "I hate pride and arrogance, evil behavior and perverse speech." They are all shades of power.

Power is dangerous because it takes rather than gives. It uses people, and when people are used up, power shoves them aside. Writers of Scripture everywhere convict power and his twin daughters pride and arrogance. Isaiah says, "The eyes of the arrogant man will be humbled and the pride of men brought low" (2:11). Isaiah returned to the theme a few chapters later: "I will put an end to the arrogance of the haughty and will humble the pride of the ruthless" (13:11). Paul wrote the Philippians: "Do nothing out of selfish ambition or vain conceit, but in humility consider others better than yourselves" (2:3). And Jesus himself said "For whoever exalts himself will be humbled, and whoever humbles himself will be exalted" (Matt 23:12).

That's the further oddity of this relationship called Christianity. Like Heraclitus, the sixth-century Ephesian philosopher who proclaimed a doctrine of constant flux ("The way up and the way down are one and the same"), Jesus tears asunder old, settled doctrines of power and truth. It had been held until Jesus's time that he who has power (Caesar, for example) spoke the truth. Indeed, in many instances the emperor was believed to be a spokesperson for the gods themselves. Talk about arrogance! But Jesus upset all that nonsense, turned it on its head. He responds to the humble. He listens to the weak and maligned. He hears the prisoner and the impoverished. He took time to play with children. Those who don't count, count with Jesus. One of the most dramatic expressions of this relationship appears in 2 Chronicles 7:14–15: "If my people, who are called by my name, will humble themselves and pray and seek my face and turn from their wicked ways, then will I hear from heaven and will forgive their sin and will heal their land. Now my eyes will be open and my ears attentive to the prayers offered in this place." Before Jesus, the powerful slink into the shadows. They are in the presence of the Creator of the universe.

Thus, we achieve the first step in our understanding of who Jesus wants us to be by the *via negativa*, by following the negative way or what the person should not be. Several negative characteristics quickly emerge: one is not to be proud; one is not to be arrogant or boasting or seeking one's own power and authority. Once establishing such traits, one discovers that a Christian being should be humble, delighting in servanthood, and pleasing to God rather than seeking the world's adulation. James nicely ties the positive qualities together, "Who is wise and understanding among you? Let him show it by his good life, by deeds done in the humility that comes from wisdom" (Jas 3:13). Similarly, Paul offers some sage advice in Philippians 2:3: "Do nothing out of selfish ambition or vain conceit, but in humility consider others better than yourselves." But, we might respond to Paul, "It's easy for you to say. Being a Super Apostle and all." Humility is a hard act to pull off. Our old selves just leak through the person that we would be, and who we really are often is just not that attractive. The old warts of pride poke through the facade. The ligaments and textures of the old self bulge tellingly against our new clothing, purchased at Redeemed, Inc.

Besides the fact that we humans find it difficult to adopt the habit of humility, the effort is also hampered by the fact that we live in perilous times for the soul. We cling to power for security against the mob. A couple of millennia ago, Paul wrote a letter where he expressed his own profound fears. In 2 Timothy 2:1–5, we find these chilling phrases: "There will be terrible times in the last days. People will be lovers of themselves, lovers of money, boastful, proud, abusive, disobedient to their parents, ungrateful, unholy, without love, unforgiving, slanderous, without self-control, brutal, not lovers of the good, treacherous, rash, conceited, lovers of pleasure rather than lovers of God—having a form of godliness but denying its power." We can paint the modern house of humankind in those colors also.

Pride, we observe, is a deadly sin, and many call it the most deadly sin. Pride is an infection. It sends its dark malignancy throughout the entire person, leaving behind the deadly viruses of envy, wrath, sloth, greed, gluttony, and lust. Pride is like long COVID; it can destroy for a lifetime. Perhaps the worst trait of pride is arrogance, an exaggerated sense of one's worth and superiority. While pride is an inward disease, arrogance is outward. It looks upon others with scorn. Arrogance dislikes and separates from a large portion of humanity.

The Christian calling, as opposed to pride and arrogance, is to humility and meekness. But with Jesus's tendency to elevate small things, we find that in humility lies our strength. As humble persons we place our trust not in ourselves but in God Almighty. Our source of strength is divine, our guide to it the Bible. Frequent Bible study is like a big booster shot of essential vitamins for the Christian; prayer is like our daily nourishment. A humble person is not necessarily weak or submissive. But the humble person is always appreciative, grateful, and caring. By such qualities humility is grounded in reality. A humble person recognizes her fundamental, God-created place in the world. Such a person truly knows herself, and thereby achieves sureness of being, the primary strength in the Lord.

Allied with humility in the house of God's strength is meekness. Now this is a confusing term. It bears the modern connotation, again, of submissiveness. As it stands against pride and arrogance, however, meekness signifies a certain set of manners that put others first. Moreover, instead of telling others what to do, meekness listens to what others have to say. When medical records were all transferred to computer files instead of paper files, it became the custom nearly everywhere for the doctor to sit in front of a computer screen while interviewing you. It is one of the most mind-boggling developments in medicine. You bare your physical body and soul to a person engrossed in a machine. It's like talking with someone who is fumbling with a smart phone. You want to plead with the person to turn it off and look at you. Instead, you find a new doctor and go out with other friends.

This thing of meekness is not being wishy-washy or weak. In fact, it shows an inner strength to really listen to someone else and to put others first. For many years I taught and profoundly admired Chaucer's *The Canterbury Tales* in the Middle English. Undaunted by what is essentially a foreign language, students from all sorts of majors and backgrounds enrolled in the course. We always stopped for a bit at the introductory lines for Chaucer's Knight:

> A Knyght ther was, and that a worthy man,
> That fro the tyme that he first bigan
> To riden out, he loved chivalrie,
> Trouthe and honour, fredom and curteisie.[1]

The knight at this time, we should remember, was the nonpareil of social strength and order. The knight was both a political and a spiritual figure. He was anointed by the archbishop but vowed allegiance to the king and carried out his will in the world. That was the task of *chivalrie*, or knighthood. What is interesting in Chaucer's description is that he lists the four elements of chivalry.

1. Trouthe is fidelity or loyalty. From it we get our English word troth.
2. Honour consists of honorable deeds.
3. Fredom is nobility, magnanimity, or generosity.
4. Courteisie is courtly manner.

If we put all these traits together, we would have a pretty good definition for meekness. And like the medieval knight, the humble person in Christendom finds strength in the One she serves.

Just a few lines following these laudatory descriptions of the Knight, establishing him as the social and spiritual leader, Chaucer heralds his meekness. Only someone as outstanding as the Knight could fully achieve the demands of the patient humility of meekness. I mention Chaucer here for a significant reason. Although *meek* has its etymology in Old Norse, it is in the Middle English *meke* that we find the roots and meaning of modern *meekness*. Now we learn that meekness is allied with the highest social paragon, that it is a quality of the highest courts, and that its qualities of noble patience and humility mark the strongest of persons. I cite Chaucer's important lines with my translation:

1. Chaucer, "Prologue," lines 43–46.

> And everemoore he hadde a sovereyn prys;
> And though that he were worthy, he was wys,
> And of his port as meeke as is a mayde.
> He nevere yet no vileynye ne sayde
> In al his lyf unto no maner wight.
> He was a verray parfit, gentil knyght.[2]
> And always he had the highest reputation;
> And even though he was eminent, he was prudent,
> And of his deportment as meek as is a maid.
> He had never uttered any villainy
> In all his life unto a person of any kind.
> He was a truly perfect, courteous knight.

There we have it. The courtly knight deports himself with the meekness of a maid, being kind and decent to every person he meets.

Finally, we should set aside the notion that it is our spiritual duty to disabuse the proud and haughty on this earth. For one thing there are just so very many of them. For another, Jesus is going to take care of that. Proverbs 16:5 promises that "The Lord detests all the proud of heart. Be sure of this: They will not go unpunished." Our task is to know God's will for us and our place in his plan. Proverbs is called "wisdom literature" not just for its pithy statements, but for this plan of a discerning life. Proverbs celebrates wisdom when it is understood as applied knowledge.

As we inquire, then, what is it to be strong in the Lord, we first pursue the *via negativa*, the path of what Christian strength is not. That permits us to rule out two qualities that the world seems to cherish: pride and arrogance. Certainly, we can add to the negative path by insisting that strength does not include, in and of itself, wealth, possessions, or large emoluments. These things are not intrinsically wrong as pride and arrogance always are. We observed, furthermore, that Christianity makes a practice of elevating small things to exemplary status. The widow's mite, the publican's prayer, the least of these receive enduring validity with Jesus. Though they may be insignificant in their own right, Jesus ennobles them and makes examples of them. Particularly in this regard, and as counters to the world's pride and arrogance, Jesus cherishes humility and meekness. In them he finds the true "strength in the Lord."

2. Chaucer, "Prologue," lines 65–73.

Jesus himself, of course, remains one of the most baffling and complex figures history has ever produced. That very fact, instead of trappings of power and prestige, makes him believable as our divine Savior. Here was a carpenter who called himself eternal God ("I tell you the truth," Jesus answered, "before Abraham was born, I am!"—John 8:58) As far as I know, Jesus is the only deity to call himself humble ("I am gentle and humble in heart"—Matthew 11:29). Furthermore, he is the only deity I have heard of to be called meek ("By the meekness and gentleness of Christ"—2 Corinthians 10:1). And, finally, Jesus is the only deity I have ever heard of that calls his followers to be meek and humble. Why? Because Jesus has not just strength but Authority. His power stretches the length of the universe, but his Authority called the universe into being.

That is the God who responds to our meekness and calls us to him.

Chapter Five

The Knight of Faith

This Present Age

THE ANTIPATHY BETWEEN SPIRITUAL faith and the clamor of culture has grown more pronounced during recent years, so much so that definitions that might set the two apart have grown blurred and indistinct. The tension has placed spiritual believers at a dangerous impasse, uncertain and febrile. In this chapter I want to examine definitions of faith, particularly in the reformed tradition, to consider a traditional "knight of faith," and to arrive at an understanding of faith in the furious swirl of contemporary culture.

One would think that there would be little confusion about faith, about its meaning or about its action. Only the most arrogant imagination could hope to improve on the elegant simplicity of Hebrews 11:1: "Now faith is being sure of what we hope for and certain of what we do not see."[1] The writer goes on to cite a chapter's worth of Old Testament examples. It would be safe to say that scores of sermons have been preached on this text, commentaries by the dozens have labored over it, and countless

1. We have a tendency to read Hebrews 11:1 and sit back on our spiritual heels, thinking that now I know the formula and am safe. Hebrews 11, however, should always be understood in the context of the preceding chapter, which stresses the urgency of getting faith right: "For in just a very little while, He who is coming will come and will not delay. But my righteous one will live by faith. And if he shrinks back, I will not be pleased with him" (10:37).

conversations have elucidated it. Emily Dickinson considered the paradox of faith in several of her poems. Perhaps the best known is the following:

> I never saw a moor,
> I never saw the sea;
> Yet know I how the heather looks,
> And what a wave must be.
> I never spoke with God,
> Nor visited in Heaven;
> Yet certain am I of the spot
> As if the chart were given.[2]

The poem is a nearly perfect commentary on Hebrews 11.

Part of the fascination with Hebrews 11:1 inheres in its beguiling simplicity. Its two parallel noun clauses serve as the objects of parallel prepositions. Its quiet linguistic beauty has at once granted its enduring appeal but also its enduring subjection to elaboration and redefinition. That is often the human way with lovely simplicity—we tend to break it into pieces to understand it.

The fact of the matter is that modern Christians, spurred by cultural influences, have gotten very adept at breaking up and tearing down faith. For some reason, some have had a compulsion, under the aegis of science, linguistics, or culture, to discredit fundamental beliefs that have shaped the Christian tradition. The greatest threats to Christian faith have never been exterior. Wars and rumors of wars, natural disasters of all sorts, upheavals in personal affairs, all often serve to strengthen faith rather than diminish it. The greater threats are often interior and insidious—the quiet whispers instead of the discordant shout. Threats to one's faith often seem to emanate from a gray, muted malaise, an ennui that settles down like a fogbank, a lackadaisical sameness to everyday life. It is a world in which we wonder what on earth we need faith for. It is also a world without wonder. As a response consider a definition of faith, largely in the Reformed tradition, and then the effects of such faith on daily life.[3]

2. Dickinson, *Final Harvest*, 236.

3. I write largely of the Reformed tradition simply because it is my own and the one I know best. Yet, it should be pointed out that the theology of faith differs little between the Reformed and Roman Catholic traditions. Aquinas stressed that two faculties are gifted by God: Reason to remove obstacles to belief and Faith to grasp the articles of belief. Aquinas develops his view most exhaustively in the "Man as Religious" section of the *Summa Theologica*. See especially *Summa* II.II.

Nearly all definitions of faith in the Reformed tradition divide into three parts: Faith is initiated by God through the Holy Spirit and the Bible; faith in the individual human is a recognition of the absolute lordship of Jesus Christ; and faith is evidenced in concrete actions. Martin Luther asserted that "Faith is a divine work in us which changes us and makes us to be born anew of God. It kills the old Adam and makes us altogether different persons, in heart and spirit and mind and powers; and it brings with it the Holy Spirit. . . . It is impossible for it not to be doing good works incessantly."[4] Luther adds that "It is impossible to separate works from faith, quite as impossible as to separate heat and light from fire."[5]

Calvin materially differs but little from Luther. In *The Institutes* he states that "We do not deny that it is the function of faith to subscribe to God's truth whenever and whatever and however it speaks."[6] Faith is actually seen as an epistemological phenomenon: "We hold faith to be a knowledge of God's will toward us, perceived from his Word" (III.ii.6). The knowledge gained, however, "consists in assurance rather than in comprehension" (III.ii.6). In one area, however, Calvin is far more emphatic than Luther. Since Calvin holds the view that humanity, in and of itself, is incapable of any good (II.ii.18–25), then he has to find a way for humanity to arrive at faith. His solution is this: Christ, when he illumines us into faith by the power of his Spirit, at the same time so engrafts us into his body that we become partakers of every good. To say that we are altogether helpless, or at best passive, in the process of faith seems to me to be erroneous—for us of course but also for Calvin. Oddly, while Calvin is keenly aware of our original sin and fallen nature, he retains a high view of human reason. He is unwilling to disregard it as a vehicle of truth. Faith shades a little differently since it resides in the heart, where the Spirit nurtures it like a little plant.

One finds that same shading, which speaks of dynamism rather than stasis, in the confessions and catechisms. The *Westminster Shorter Confession* contains language similar to what we have seen: "The grace of faith, whereby the elect are enabled to believe to the saving of their souls, is the work of the Spirit of Christ in their hearts; and is ordinarily wrought by the ministry of the Word: by which also, and the administration of the sacraments, and prayer, it is increased and strengthened."[7] *The Belgic*

4. Luther, *Luther's Works, Vol. 35: Word and Sacrament I*, 370.
5. Luther, *Luther's Works, Vol. 35: Word and Sacrament I*, 371.
6. Calvin, *Institutes*, III.ii.7. Further quotations will be cited parenthetically.
7. Ch. 10, 4.

Confession, moreover, states: "We believe that . . . the Holy Spirit kindles in our hearts an upright faith which embraces Jesus Christ with all His merits, appropriates Him, and seeks nothing more besides Him."[8] Finally, the venerable *Heidelberg Catechism* holds that "True faith is not only a sure knowledge, whereby I hold for truth all that God has revealed to us in his Word, but also a firm confidence that the Holy Spirit works in my heart by the gospel."[9]

We may conclude from the tradition then (and minor works affirm what these documents assert) that faith is a gift of Jesus working through the Holy Spirit in humans to grow human relationships with God. Even while confessing that, however, many in the Reformed tradition are a bit leery of giving up control to the Holy Spirit. Contemporary believers in particular remain pragmatic. Technology and the Holy Spirit rarely share the same rooms. In his *Ethical Reflections*, Henry Stob observes that "The lofty God of Calvinism is not a God into whose presence one enters boldly or with whom one associates on easy and intimate terms; mysticism can hardly grow on Calvinist soil."[10] But there is a point to be made here, and it may be solved by arguing that faith is a reciprocating process between human and God. As we reach out to God (by contemplation, by reading God's word, by attending holy services, for example) God through his Holy Spirit reaches out to us, informing us of our salvation in Jesus Christ. It is not an "if/then" construction, but rather one of merciful simultaneity. It is a mystery we accept at the altar of worship.

One further thing must be said about defining faith. Examining certain biblical passages carefully, one quickly becomes aware that faith is not merely a method for how one comes to know Christ; rather, it is a way of living. Romans 1:17 states the case: "For in the gospel a righteousness from God is revealed, a righteousness that is by faith from first to last, just as it is written: 'The righteous will live by faith.'" And that being the case, it is no easily discernible way, but one all too often fraught with uncertainty and conflict. It is a way that led Jonah to Nineveh, via a whale's belly. It led Rahab to place the lives of her whole family on a length of scarlet cord. It led Esther to parade before King Xerxes to save the Jews. Faith costs something.[11]

8. Article 22.

9. 7.21.

10. Stob, *Ethical Reflections*, 52.

11. In his study of the *Heidelberg Catechism*, Kevin De Young sees a danger in acts of

For that reason alone, perhaps, the verses of James 2 are so daunting to modern theologians and Christians. James insists that the only way to validate faith is to act upon it. In 2:17 he states, "Faith by itself, if it is not accompanied by action, is dead." And in verse 24: "You see that a person is justified by what he does and not by faith alone." As if that is not enough, James states in verse 26: "As the body without the spirit is dead, so faith without deeds is dead." We moderns do not like verses like that. We do not like being told what to do, or even to do something. We like comfort and assurance. Now we have this James fellow telling us that our faith is not enough.

And what exactly is it that I have to do?

We look for models, sure and certain guides, to test our actions. One such that the Bible holds before us repeatedly is Abraham, sometimes called the "father of the faith." It was because Abraham was willing to do the impossible, to enact the unimaginable, and live with the unforgiveable. Like that Lamborghini Venmo Roadster I desire—for an afternoon only—Abraham seems so very far past my reality as to be the stuff of myth. Abraham does not merely walk in faith; he incarnates faith, risking the awful unholy so that he may be found holy. Dallas Willard writes with admiration, "Abraham, the man of faith, went out not knowing where he was going. That was not a blind leap of faith, because Abraham knew God. He *knew* God. He didn't know where he was going, but he knew he was going with God."[12] And I respond with vast trepidation, if Abraham is God's favored one, then I and most everyone I know don't stand a chance of divine favor. His heroism is too huge. His faith too . . . too outlandishly faithful. One wonders: is Abraham paradigm or paradox? Perhaps those were the exact qualities that led Søren Kierkegaard to designate Abraham as the ideal "knight of faith." And in our dangerously muddled times, can he serve as such once again?

When Søren Kierkegaard died in November, 1855, few people noticed and even fewer people mourned. He was, for all practical purposes, an enigma, an anomaly. He was, in thought, word, and deed, a stranger in his own land.

A large part of his self-proclaimed mission was to attack the rigidity and narrowness of the Danish State Church. It was not the way to win friends and influence people. One might rightly say that no one in Denmark

---

faith: "What we don't want are Christians who admirably try to relieve suffering in the world, but are indifferent toward eternal suffering." *Good News We Almost Forgot*, 37.

12. Willard, *Allure of Gentleness*, 169.

much cared for him, including his fiancée Regine Olsen; Kierkegaard broke off his relationship with her to devote more time to writing. Writing books, often under pseudonyms, that hardly anybody read or understood. And when he died, the books were quickly forgotten.

So it remained, a painful footnote in history's annals, until a century or so later when Kierkegaard's books and thoughts enjoyed a revival. During the 1960s, surely in America and probably in Denmark too, the church once again seemed to lose a large degree of its relevance. Doubts were fueled by the *Time* cover story of April 8, 1966, wondering "Is God Dead?" In such a way, a movement known as the death of God theologians was founded, announcing that God no longer has authority over us and that the sacred has disappeared in society. On its heels religion was banned in the classrooms, universities became citadels of atheism and scientism, and young people spaced out at Woodstock as Grace Slick and Jefferson Airplane blasted "White Rabbit" with its clarion call to "feed your head." Stoned young people sprawled in the mud. People wondered whether Christianity would survive, and if so, what form it would take. *Faith* was just a word we used to use.

Kierkegaard had answered a century before that it was a Christianity of radical personal faith, often opposed to the rational treatises of doctrinal religion, by which we survived. In fact, the organized church might call this faith "absurd" simply because it refused to capitulate to traditional categories of truth. In particular, Kierkegaard's slim volume *Fear and Trembling*, initially published under a pseudonym, became one of the most important books of the time.

Kierkegaard tells the story of Abraham, trudging up Mount Moriah with Isaac, intending to sacrifice his son. He did so, Kierkegaard points out, in defiance of all established and rational norms of his age. While such institutions as religion, politics, society, and such would declare the intended act to be murder, Abraham proceeded on faith alone. He couldn't see it, but he believed God would provide. Thus, Kierkegaard calls Abraham his "knight of faith."[13]

13. It should be clear, if one reads the entirety of *Fear and Trembling* carefully, that Kierkegaard is less concerned with Abraham as a man of faith than he is with Abraham as an existential hero, an example of the individual particular surpassing the ethical universal. In fact, Kierkegaard states near the book's conclusion that "Faith's paradox is this, that the single individual is higher than the universal, that the single individual . . . determines his relation to the universal through his relation to the absolute." *Fear and Trembling*, 97.

Having come of age during the 1960s, I did not have to work hard to generate sympathy for Kierkegaard. I was blessed to attend a top-notch Christian college, where reading any kind of philosophy was encouraged. The books we were reading on our own, when true education takes place, were by Kierkegaard, Nietzsche, Camus, Sartre, and that ilk. We often felt captive to a mindless machine that ruled our lives, especially when we went to renew our 2S deferments to stay out of the draft. But Abraham as a knight of faith? Even then that was a little hard for me to swallow. Maybe the sole place of Abraham in the Bible is to show what God can do with a seriously flawed piece of humanity.

Abraham's difficulties started when he was seventy-five-year-old Abram, and he and Sarai (ten years younger) and a few hangers-on like Lot left behind their family in Haran and traipsed down to Shechem. There was a famine going on there, so they just kept going until they wound up in Egypt. The problem there was that Sarai had a fatal flaw—she was stunningly beautiful. Abram was afraid that Pharaoh would spot her and want her in his harem. For Pharaoh to do that, he simply killed the spouse. That's what pharaohs do. Fearful of his own demise, Abram told Sarai to pretend she was his sister. That way, when Pharaoh took her (which did not seem to bother Abram a whole lot) Abram would escape alive.

Abram didn't seem to have a whole lot of steel in his spine. He bartered his wife for a good meal in Egypt. As a matter of fact, he liked the ploy of pawning off Sarai as his sister so much he repeated it a few years later with King Abimelech.

And then of course we come to the humdinger. Abraham is required to sacrifice Sarah's only son, Isaac. Abraham had a prior son with Hagar, but he had let jealous Sarah drive them into the wilderness. Life seemed cheap in those days. The familiar story here is nearly a tragicomedy. Abraham trudges along to Mount Moriah with Isaac at his side. Doesn't poor Isaac wonder for a second where they are going? Then Abraham chops some wood and lays it on the back of Isaac. Later he will lay Isaac back on the wood. Abraham actually raises the knife, fully intent on murdering Isaac, before the Lord stays his arm. I know the theological archetypes that come to the fore here. Indeed, Jesus was the sacrifice upon the wood of the cross while his Father stood by. Yes, God himself provided himself as the sacrifice.

Exegete the passage until you're blue in the face. It doesn't help me much. If I, in my fallen clay, had stood in Abraham's place, I would have refused to go. I would rather face the fires of hell for my disobedience than kill one of my children. Kierkegaard rightly called the event *absurd*, meaning that it made no rational sense.

I have a difficult time seeing Abraham as a hero of the Old Testament or as a knight of faith. I find myself paging through Scripture looking for alternatives. I wonder who does embody those heroic traits of the knight of faith. I readily find candidates. I have always been fascinated, for example, by stubborn Jonah, who lived on second chances. Lovely Hadassah, according to legend one of the three most beautiful women who ever lived (with Eve and Mary), was also a powerhouse politician who lifted her people from a sentence of death. Saint John, living in lonely exile and pestered by visions that he knew to be true, has always intrigued me. Ezra and Nehemiah strike me as a two-for-one deal on heroes. But I finally stop at an unlikely place. That human-all-too-human man by the name of Job.

To fully understand Job, though, I have to flip ahead to the New Testament and consider Jesus's distinction between two kinds of peace. After a lengthy address to his disciples, including the revelation of trouble and suffering to come, Jesus promises them that the Father will send to them the Holy Spirit. Thereby they will experience a divine peace that the world cannot overcome. In promising this peace, Jesus contrasts it with worldly peace that is dependent upon things and events. There is a peace which surpasses things and events; yes, that surpasses understanding. Thus, Jesus delivers the promise that "Peace I leave with you; my peace I give to you; not as the world gives do I give to you. Let not your hearts be troubled, neither let them be afraid" (John 14:27). This distinction gains clarity through the story of a man who lived in a land with the strange-sounding name of Uz.

He was a good man. He loved God and he abhorred evil. In his righteous walk with God, God blessed him. Seven sons and three daughters he had. Thousands of sheep, camels, and oxen. The family had expansive feasts in their spacious house. And the man thanked God for his blessing and remained faithful to God. There was peace in his house.

Until a certain day when Satan, going to and fro on the earth, saw this man Job and wanted to destroy his peacefulness. This is what Satan does. Since he is the one who broke peace with God, and since his separation from peace is eternal, Satan's worldly work is to destroy the peace of the believer. He thought Job a worthy adversary. He wanted to tempt him. and he acquired the Lord's permission to do so.

From our point in history, of course, we remember that once before God had permitted Satan to tempt Eve and Adam, in the garden of

Eden. There too the peace of that fair garden was shattered. It took Jesus's blood to revoke the curse. The drama on Job's doorstep had truly cosmic ramifications.

Like another Adam, this man is tested. One by one the messengers ran panting to his door with terrible news. An enemy struck and slaughtered the oxen. Fire from heaven devoured the sheep and the shepherds. The camels are slain, along with their keepers. And then this woeful message: a windstorm struck the eldest son's house, killing all of Job's sons and daughters.

The Eden-broken peace is broken again. Surely this man has cause to rail against God. Why me, Lord? But we read this instead: "In all this Job did not sin or charge God with wrong" (Job 1:22).

Job wasn't asked to climb a mountain. He didn't labor up the flanks of a hill with a small boy panting by his side, his knife tucked into the sash around his waist. Job was asked to be there—to stand still in a world where all is whirling and askew, friends whispering in his ears that this is all folly. He bent his head and was . . . Job. Nothing more.

But there is more to come.

The affliction thus far has been external—a loss of possessions and family. Now the destruction is directed at Job's own body. From the soles of his feet to the crown of his head, Job breaks out in "loathsome" sores. His body is so riddled with painful affliction, such a torment of the flesh, that his friends don't even recognize him. This is a hurt one cannot escape. Every inch of Job's body is caught in a fiery crucible of pain. At last Job feels utterly cast out, and at last the words of cursing come to his lips: "Let the day perish wherein I was born" (Job 3:3).

No angelic visitor has informed Job why he is suffering. No promise has been made to him that the suffering will soon pass away. His world is simply and abruptly turned from peace to terror, from happiness to sorrow, from joy to torment. Job is living evidence of the words of Paul: "For we are not contending against flesh and blood, but against the principalities, against the powers, against the world rulers of this present darkness, against the spiritual hosts of wickedness in the heavenly places" (Eph 6:12). Job is in the eye of a maelstrom of divine warfare, and he can scarcely understand his battle plan. He knows only too well, though, that his peace has been shattered, apparently beyond reason, beyond belief, beyond restoration.

Job has three friends who come to comfort him—Eliphaz, Bildad, and Zophar. Eliphaz, perhaps the most sympathetic and compassionate of Job's friends, encourages him to lean on God's mercy and remain steadfast in his struggle. But Job's wounds are beyond the touch of such encouragement. How can there be any good, Job wonders, when everything appears to be going bad? What reason can one find to go on living when such unreasonable things happen? When the mind fumbles with clumsy fingers for the hand of God, what clear answers emerge? No, Job replies to Eliphaz, the peace is broken. What can I mean to God who has forsaken me?

Then Bildad speaks, suggesting that if Job cannot find firm assurance by looking to the future, then perhaps he can learn from the past. Surely Job has seen God's hand in the past, Bildad argues; shouldn't that be sufficient assurance for the present? Job, however, wonders what answers he can find now, sitting in the dust, devastated and in pain. Who can understand what God is doing *now*, and the loathing Job has for his life *now*? *Now* is "the land of gloom and chaos, where light is as darkness" (Job 10:22). When one suffers in darkness, it is hard to see any light filtering down from the past or any glimpse ahead into the future.

We easily sympathize with Job's feelings. Almost every Christian, at one time or another, has walked along the edge of that spiritual loneliness that so overwhelms Job. Sometimes Job seems like a spiritual brother and his desolation seems our desolation. Job despairs of ever seeing spiritual light again. The darkness has overwhelmed him, and he seems to be fumbling in tight little circles that close more and more narrowly upon him.

How devastating it must be, then, when Job's third friend Zophar simply loses patience with his state. Zophar was born bereft of empathy; he is the pragmatist in the group. Relying on shock therapy rather than sympathy, Zophar wonders why Job can't just snap out of it. Zophar's advice still echoes down the hallways of our contemporary churches. In Zophar's mind, Job is hiding some secret sin that he must confess. It's like the tired cliche: What's *really* wrong with you? Get rid of the sin and get right with God. Toughen up and get over it.

How nice it would be if a person could simply get a spiritual injection that would cure a suffering such as Job's. Or perhaps get a vaccine that would prevent it altogether. But there are no quick and easy cures for Job. He cannot just "snap out of it."

Evidently Job's friends are well-intentioned, and a degree of truth inheres in each of the things they say. Yes, Eliphaz, one does have to lean on God's mercy. But sometimes one doesn't even have the strength to lean. Think of Job, sprawled in the dust. And yes, Bildad, one does take solace from past blessings and from a future hope. But can't something be done about this present darkness? See Job, scratching at his bleeding sores, head to toe. Yes, Zophar, our hard-nosed pragmatist, one does have to battle against the darkness. But what can Job do when it seems that he is pinned down, hardly able to breathe, limbs like water? A degree of truth appears in each suggestion, but each is finally insufficient. Why?

Because each focuses upon Job, and is dependent upon his action. Each sees the answer coming from Job to God, when the answer comes from God to Job. The lesson of Job is identical to that recorded in Ephesians 2:8–9: "For by grace you have been saved through faith; and this is not our own doing, it is the gift of God—not because of works, lest any man should boast." Our peace begins and ends in God's will and, although we will work within that will, our peace is not of our own doing but from God alone. Job's response to these three philosophies marks him as a true hero of faith. Even affirming that he can find no answers, that he has been struck down without fault, and that his own suffering is insurmountable, Job makes a soaring assertion of faith.

Job is remarkably candid in his struggle as it is narrated in the nineteenth chapter. He readily acknowledges his "errors," but assures his friends that they are his concern alone. Moreover, he claims he calls out for help into a silent universe. He feels there is no divine justice. If Job laments his forsaken spiritual estate, he deplores his sickly physical condition: "I am nothing but skin and bones; I have escaped with only the skin of my teeth" (19:20). He pleads for pity, not for philosophies. Faced with pain and a silent universe, Job nonetheless makes one of the most powerful testaments of faith recorded in Scripture:

> I know that my Redeemer lives,
> and that in the end he will stand
> upon the earth.
> And after my skin has been destroyed,
> yet in my flesh I will see God. (19:25–26)

Like an elegant stage master, with unparalleled timing, the young man Elihu enters the scene to proclaim the absolute power and majesty of God. A whirlwind descends, apt prelude to the voice of God which silences all voices:

> Where were you when I laid the foundation of the earth?
> Tell me, if you have understanding.

> Who determined its measurements—surely you know!
> Or who stretched the line upon it?
> On what were its bases sunk,
> Or who laid its cornerstone,
> When the morning stars sang together,
> And all the sons of God shouted for joy?
> (38:4–7)

The wonderful irony of God's questions is that they are beyond answering by Job's questioners.

The voice of God does not always come out of the whirlwind or from a burning bush or from the mountaintop. Sometimes it comes, as to Elijah, in a still, small voice saying simply, I am God and I am here. But therein lies the believer's peace. The Lord of heaven and earth, the Maker of Light, still reigns in our darkness.

In that last phrase lies the key to understanding Job and also the warrant for him as a knight of faith. Out of the darkness, Job asserted his faith. In the moment of confusion and uncertainty, he declared his belief. When all he knew was loss and emptiness, he found someone to believe in.

The troubled story of Job has a happy ending. When Job turns to God, God restores his fortune. He is blessed in the latter days beyond his former days. But the restoration of fortune is beside the point of the story. The turning to God is what mattered, and that applies equally to us. Because the Maker of Light entered the deepest gulf of our darkness when he died on Calvary, we have an eternal light to guide our way. Because Jesus walked among humans and said "Peace, be still," we have a peacemaker to lighten our path. Every Christian's story has a happy ending. That is the promise of his perfect peace to those whose hearts are stayed in him.

And, finally, how about Kierkegaard, his mind's eye riveted upon the bent figure of old Abraham, steadfastly trying to do his best to do God's will while not understanding a bit of it? In fact, Abraham walked toward Mount Moriah in defiance of everything he had learned of God's will. He not only dared the impossible, but he also dared the impermissible. While we understand that Kierkegaard himself was uneasy in the ironclad dictates of the state church, and while we understand that his father's brutal catechetical training of him during his youth wounded him deeply, we also understand that Kierkegaard held a deeply profound appreciation for faith in God while living in a disturbing and trying civilization.

There is little definitive information about the exceedingly odd "Epilogue" that Kierkegaard furnished for *Fear and Trembling*. It wanders from the spice market in the Netherlands to Heraclitus standing by his flowing river. In its brief passage, however, Kierkegaard twice remarks that "Faith is the highest passion in a human being."[14] Kierkegaard confesses that he has far to go yet in his own life. Faith is believing in the face of a disbelieving and scoffing age. It acknowledges not a relative truth—"this is true because 51 out of 100 people believe it's true"—but that there is one absolute truth. That voice is once again worth listening to.

Abraham left the daily confines of his life. He went out; more, he climbed up. How solitary with all traditional guides to truth falling away behind him. Abraham sought the truth utterly alone. As he went, unless his mind were a dense clod of insensate matter, terrors and questions must have tormented him. Yes, a knight of faith. But Job—he was afflicted right where he lived, in the midst of everything that gave comfort, meaning, and hope. All the structures, all the props he had built his life upon, were blown away in a gust of storm. Then the pollution of evil crawled inside him, abraded the delicate nerve endings, broke the skin in purple lesions. He dug at his flesh with a shattered slice of a broken pot. Blood sluiced trails across his skin. But Job had faith that his Lord would prevail. Yes, a knight of faith.

14. Kierkegaard, *Fear and Trembling*, 146.

Chapter Six

The Dragon and the Lion

The Nature of Hope

In 1 Corinthians 13:13 we find, and have probably memorized, the sacred triad of theological virtues: "And now these three remain: faith, hope and love. But the greatest of these is love." So familiar are the words that we tend to pass over them with a nod of acknowledgment and not much more. Reflecting upon them, however, brings some troubling thoughts to mind. For example, love and faith seem thoroughly amplified in Scripture. Implications are accounted for; the fullness of each in God amply spoken for. But hope somehow seems to be the runt of the litter, the one not thoroughly developed in Scripture, the one that puzzles.

The word *hope* appears often enough, but it is most frequently used as an indifferent expectation. When friends part, or when a writer closes a letter, he or she might say, "I hope to see you soon." Most often that is also how the word appears in Scripture. It leads one to wonder, What is so great about hope anyway? Does it merit its place in the divine triad along with faith and love?

If one searches diligently, the Bible supplies additional uses of hope, although, again, it often seems an added or passing thought. For example, Job says, "Oh, that I might have my request, that God would grant what I hope for" (6:8). What Job hopes for at this point is annihilation, so his hope, here seen as a desperate wish, hardly thought out, isn't likely to be granted. We see another and more familiar use of the word in Psalm 25:5: "Guide me in your ways, O Lord, teach me your paths; for my hope is in you." Here hope carries a sense of trust and dependence—as if to say, "You are my one and only hope for life." This is the meaning that Peter apparently had in mind when he wrote, "He has given us new birth into a living hope through the resurrection of Jesus Christ from the dead " (1 Pet 1:3).

One other scriptural use of hope appears. It is usually neglected, unfortunately so for it is vital. In fact, I will spend the rest of this chapter examining its implications. It has much to say about the nature of our age and about who and what we are as Christians: that is, hope as longing.[1] The biblical imprimatur occurs in just four brief verses. The writer of Psalm 119 is consumed with love for God's law and the whole, long poem is a paean to it. In verse 20 the psalmist writes, "My soul is consumed with longing for your laws at all times." In verse 81, the longing is openly associated with hope: "My soul faints with longing for your salvation, but I have put my hope in your word."

Two passages from the New Testament amplify this sense of hope as longing, or a deep, unsettled yearning. Neither one of these actually uses the word *hope*. They do, however, describe well the yearning that lies at the heart of Christian hope. The writer of Hebrews pauses in the pantheon of heroes of faith in chapter 11 and writes: "All these people were still living by faith when they died. They did not receive the things promised; they only saw them and welcomed them from a distance. And they admitted that they were aliens and strangers on earth" (11:13). Hope bears this strong sense of life being unsettled, that these are shadowlands we live in and there is a deeper, brighter world to come. In his letter to the Philippians, Paul summarizes all that Jesus has done for his people, then expresses his longing to be with his Savior. He writes, "Forgetting what is behind and straining toward what is ahead, I press on toward the goal to win the prize for which God has called me heavenward in Christ Jesus" (Phil 3:13–14). That "pressing on", that straining toward a goal, that longing and yearning for it, is what we mean by hope in Christianity.

Or do we? For it seems that hope in contemporary Christendom has dwindled to murmurs. Hope has been supplanted by a host of political and social issues that cry out for the church's full attention. How did this

1. John Calvin discusses hope with this meaning of expectation or longing in mind: "Hope is no other than an expectation of things which faith has believed to be truly promised by God. . . . Faith is the foundation on which hope rests, hope nourishes and sustains faith" (*Institutes*, III.ii.42). For Calvin, hope functions as something of a handmaiden to faith.

happen, and how can genuine hope be recovered as an integral, celebrated part of our faith? To answer that requires looking at shifting worldviews of the last two centuries.

Many thinkers trace the genesis of our modern spiritual malaise to the Enlightenment, a movement dominating the eighteenth century. It stressed mind over matter, the supremacy of reason, and the celebration of rational analysis in scientific method. And, yes, the diminishment of religion. The clarion call of such beliefs was sounded by David Hume in his influential *An Enquiry Concerning Human Understanding*, which included the famous essay "On Miracles." There Hume debunked not only miracles but also all claims about Christ on the grounds of insufficient evidence: "Our Evidence, then, for the Truth of the Christian Religion is less than the Evidence for the Truth of our Senses." He adds that "A wise Man, therefore, proportions his Belief to the Evidence."[2] The essay thereby typifies the supremacy of the scientific method and the elevation of reason over belief during the Enlightenment.

Those qualities endure into our age. If anything, they are accentuated. Scientific method has hardened into technological miracles, in which many now place their faith. Wonders are now performed daily in hospital operating rooms. Marvels stun us with each new edition of smart phones, which increase yearly in smartness until their intelligence now seems to rule over our lives.

Although the modern mind is much indebted to the Enlightenment, the modern soul is more indebted to its successor, Romanticism, a school of thought that prevailed over much of the nineteenth century. As a literary and philosophical movement, as well as a world and life view, it is difficult to overstate the effects of Romanticism upon our own age, even if one is not fully aware of it. For example, the Enlightenment placed human intellect on the throne of the universe and did away with God. Romanticism experienced this loss with a devastating sadness and weariness. The fact that it celebrated sensations largely negated the strides that the intellect had made in the previous century. Wordsworth couldn't have put it any more clearly:

> Sweet is the lore which Nature brings;
> Our meddling intellect
> Mis-shapes the beauteous forms of things;—
> We murder to dissect.[3]

2. Hume, "On Miracles," Section X, Pt. 1.
3. Wordsworth, "Tables Turned," 190.

For the Romantics, any experience in nature, however brief and intense, is far more inspiring of knowledge than hours spent in a laboratory.

Importantly then, rational scrutiny diminishes in subservience to experience, nature, and sensations. Still, the Romantic mood is marked everywhere by an intense longing, a desire to know and experience ultimate things. Romantic paintings, for example and of the type we see by Bierstadt, Cole, and Durand, often dissipate in an intense mystic haze in the background. This often represented the furthest limits of the artist's imagination, that point beyond which, in his mortal chains, he cannot go.

To fully understand the effects of Romanticism on our age, it is helpful to pause briefly with the traits of Romanticism that originated in German literature. These developed simultaneously with the Romantic movements in England, America, and indeed across Europe. Germany birthed three items in particular, all of which marked Romanticism generally and all of which will help us understand Christian hope in our own time. Each of these schools of thought coined key terms that have entered our modern world and life vocabulary.

The first of these terms is *sehnsucht*, commonly translated as "yearning" or "longing." It comes from a poem by Goethe that appears in his 1795 novel *Wilhelm Meister's Apprenticeship*.[4] Its influence was enormous; in fact, the poem itself has been set to music by such composers as Beethoven, Schumann, and Tchaikovsky. Its first stanza follows with my translation:

Nur wer die Sehsucht kennt	Only those who know yearning
Weiss, was ich leide!	Know what gives me sorrow!
Allein und abgetrennt	Alone and separated
Von aller Freude.	From all joy.

This sense of unattainable longing, of a yearning for something abstract and beyond the pale of this life, characterized all later Romanticism.

Two other German literary works had a substantial influence on the growth of Romanticism. The first was the so-called "Quest of the Blue Flower," similar to *sehnsucht* in that it sought the unobtainable, pure ideal. The concept originated in a work by the writer known as Novalis. *Heinrich von Ofterdingen* thinly masked Novalis's love for Sophie, an ideal woman as rare as the blue flower. When Novalis died, the work was completed by his friend Ludwig Tieck and published in 1801, at the birth of German Romanticism.

4. Goethe, *Wilhelm Meister's Apprenticeship*, Bk. 2.

The final term unique to German Romanticism, but with an equally large influence, was *weltschmerz*, which may be translated as a "painful world," or more colloquially as "world-weariness." The term was coined by the writer Jean Paul in his novel *Selina* (1827). Remember that the Romantics sought an ideal world. Consequently, when they had to deal with this present reality where Nature is besmirched and even young people sicken and die, it was a painful ordeal. It exacerbated the longing of *sennsucht* or for the blue flower.

Most literary scholars agree that it is impossible to provide a narrow definition of Romanticism. Instead, they speak of "shared qualities" or "common traits." So those above—longing, a quest for meaning, and world weariness—function as a starting point. Romantics also speak of a renewed appreciation for those common things ignored by the Enlightenment. There is a shift in sensibility, in what things to value. The consequence in Romantic poetry is that writers felt a freedom to write on any common thing as if it had infinite worth. Thus, Wordsworth wrote poems celebrating a beggar and a cuckoo bird. Coleridge topped them all by writing the poem "To a Young Ass":

> Poor little Foal of an oppressed race!
> I love the languid patience of thy face.
> And oft with gentle hand I give thee bread
> And clap thy ragged coat, and pat thy head.[5]

Not only did the Romantics not mind writing such poems, they positively gloried in it. In larger terms, though, such works show a turning to things of this life. The Enlightenment held that if you didn't think great thoughts, you didn't count for much. The thinking human was their ideal. The Romantic writers, on the other hand, were aware of the importance and the value of even the smallest, most slighted things in life.

The conflict has much to say about hope in modern life. The all-consuming silence about hope in our time is a direct result of the Enlightenment glorification of the individual mind and the pressure for results now. "Immediacy" is the banner word for much of our contemporary technology. Longing or yearning seems almost foolish. While Romantics lamented the disappearance of small things, in the vacuum writers gloried in the celebration of self. Romanticism paved the way for a writer like Friedrich Nietzsche, who in 1891 wrote: "Who is the great dragon whom

5. Coleridge, "To a Young Ass," 138.

the spirit will no longer call lord and god? 'Thou shalt' is the name of the great dragon. But the spirit of the lion says, 'I will.'"[6] On the threshold of the twentieth century, Nietzsche introduced the lordship of the individual. The gods have disappeared.

But Nietzsche could not get rid of Christianity quite that easily. In fact, as the assailing forces arrayed against Christianity only strengthened in the twentieth century, Christian hope seemed to beat louder in the breasts of believers. It had to. We endured two world wars, a host of lesser wars, the Spanish Flu of 1918, the rise of nuclear power and the dropping of nuclear bombs, and the invention of more gizmos than any one person could enumerate. The whole twentieth century was an endurance race, and as we staggered into the twenty-first, we wondered how we survived.

I went to graduate school during the tumultuous 1960s, the historical fulcrum from a settled way of life to one steeped in whiplash change, dark uncertainty, and random experimentation. Perhaps because of the terrible tumult, many young people were hoping for something better—just better than what we had. But every new voice promising something better was silenced by the tumult itself. Martin Luther King Jr. exhorted us to a new dream, but he was slain in Memphis. Bobby Kennedy promised peace now, and he was gunned down in a hotel lobby. And the thunder in the distant hills growled that there was a war going on and Uncle Sam was coming to get you. He found me right in that tidy classroom, picked me up with dirty nails, and plopped me down in a jungle where things went boom in the night. And the day.

We aptly trace the trajectory of the twentieth century by its wars; it was full of them. When it became time for me to write a thesis for my master's degree, I searched my meager stock of ideas and decided I would write on Romantic longing. It seemed appropriate to the time. Goethe's *sehnsucht*, Ludwig Tieck's "quest for the blue flower," Keats's Grecian Urn, the world-weariness all seemed very much a part of the spirit of the age. I remember nothing about the final form of that thesis, because by the time it was graded and my invitation to continue for the PhD came, I was on a stretch-DC-9, winging westward over the Pacific, with 209 other G.I.s.

Another fair and certain way to measure the evolution of the twentieth century was through its music. The early decades, despite two world wars, were dominated by swing, ragtime, and big band orchestras. They celebrated a showman named Liberace, replaced at the end of the century by the Rocket

6. Nietzsche, *Zarathustra*, 26–27.

Man himself, Elton John. Smack in the middle, the sunny 1950s saw the birth of rock and roll and the celebration of frivolous things. The Top Forty charts held titles like "Lucille," "Hound Dog," "Earth Angel," "Blue Suede Shoes," "Great Balls of Fire," "La Bamba," "All Shook Up," "Blueberry Hill," "Rock Around the Clock," "Fever," and "Sixteen Tons." Really, what kind of angst can one have when "All I Have to Do is Dream"? In the 1960s, however, we have "The Sound of Silence." While we pondered the desolate but mellifluous lyrics of that song, we were lulled by its delicious melody. Roy Orbison wailed "Only the Lonely" and Leslie Gore declared "It's my party and I'll cry if I want to." A group called Procol Harum bewildered everyone with the mysterious, mesmerizing lyrics of "A Whiter Shade of Pale." Dozens, literally dozens, of songs celebrated drug use of various kinds, and Grace Slick and Jefferson Airplane closed Woodstock and the decade in 1969 by singing a spine-tingling "White Rabbit," with the anthem, "Feed your head, feed your head." It's what the dormouse said.

If music is one way of defining an era, as I believe it was during the 1960s, then two songs in particular signal the cultural upheaval. On June 5, 1968, songwriter Dick Holler was working in New York when he received the news that Bobby Kennedy had been slain. He claimed that he went home and wrote the haunting lyrics of "Abraham, Martin, and John" in ten minutes. Although several artists covered the song, Dion DiMucci had the popular hit:

> Has anybody here seen my old friend Bobby
> Can you tell me where he's gone
> I thought I saw him walkin' up over the hill
> With Abraham, Martin, and John.[7]

And that was the picture left in our minds: the four dead heroes walking away from us.

The other major hit that reflected the history and spirit of the 1960s was "American Pie," by Don McLean. Ostensibly, the 1971 song memorialized the deaths of Buddy Holly, Ritchie Valens, and the Big Bopper (J. P. Richardson) in a plane crash in 1959. The genius of the song, however, is that for its many minutes (eight minutes, forty-two seconds) one disconnected allusion to the past after the other followed in quick succession. Across the US, Canada, England, Australia, and other lands where the

7. Dion Dimucci, *Abraham Martin and John*, by Dick Holler. Laurie Records, 1968.

song hit the top of the charts, people gathered to discuss and decipher the lines of the song. It was a cultural phenomenon.

I believe that we live in the legacy of the 1960s yet today. The era evoked a deep distrust of all things governmental. It listened to Timothy Leary, who told young people to just turn on and tune out. The era brought a thorough disillusionment with the established churches, many of which supported the war in southeast Asia. Students held universities hostage and burned buildings on their campuses. Inner cities rose in flames and whole blocks collapsed in ash. Several generations now have been taught that they are answerable only to themselves. With the emergence of this existential ethics, punishment or even wrongdoing became a foreign vocabulary. Individual foibles, frolics, and misdemeanors are just part of living life to the fullest. Hell disappeared from Western culture as a topic of serious concern.

The latest incarnation of the absence of God also achieved new emphasis during the 1960s with the so-called "death of God theologians." They were prominent young scholars, most of them of theology, teaching at such institutions as Harvard, Syracuse, Temple, and Emory Universities. They gave many license to throw their faith aside, along with all its moral oughts and shalt nots. In *The Disappearance of God*, published in 1965, J. Hillis Miller wrote: "When the old system of symbols binding man to God has finally evaporated man finds himself alone and in spiritual poverty. Modern times begin when man confronts his isolation, his separation from everything outside himself."[8]

In the absence of legitimate answers from religion, we attempt to satiate ourselves with gimmickry. Health clubs abound on every corner, but obesity levels simultaneously reach an all-time high. Astronomical lottery prizes pander to the endless itch for money. They are all snags concocted by skilled marketers of course, but they work to make us believe that "hope" is an outmoded commodity. We may have longed for something like heaven once upon a time of fairy tales, but it is time now to wake up to the real world of here and now, of heaven on earth through technology, money, medicine, and Prevagen.

We presently live in the legacy of two centuries of revolution. But it seems that all of humanity's grand schemes have backfired, and we now stand alone and lonely in a darkening world. Miller observed that "We are alienated from God; we have alienated ourselves from nature; we are alienated from our fellow men; and, finally, we are alienated from ourselves, the

8. Miller, *Disappearance of God*, 7.

buried life we never seem able to reach. The result is a radical sense of inner nothingness."[9] The Enlightenment gave us the lordship of man thinking, but we understand that not all his thoughts have been wise. The bright seeds of Romanticism were planted in a vague, unsettled yearning, but humans had little sense of just what they longed for. A better life? That sounds sensible, but all too often the Romantics just stand there yearning. For what is not exactly clear. The quest of the blue flower? Even if we find it, it will probably be artificial, made in China. While surveying the present state of humanity in *The Abolition of Man*, C. S. Lewis proclaims the advent of "Men Without Chests." He writes: "We make men without chests and expect of them virtue and enterprise. We laugh at honour and are shocked to find traitors in our midst. We castrate and bid the geldings be fruitful."[10]

But finally, in our present time it seems like even nature has conspired against us. When humans start manipulating nature, we get things like COVID-19, with approximately 1,200,000 deaths in the US and over 7,000,000 worldwide. While each new hurricane exceeds the last in causing damage and deaths, California burns to the ground in its own funeral pyre and the Midwest shrivels in drought. But it's not very fruitful to elaborate all the ways we are destroying the planet and ourselves. We can hardly escape such knowledge, and no one appears able to do much about our headstrong slide into oblivion. We are the victims of our own crimes, and there is no hope for another liberator to bring answers. Unfortunately, we have lost touch for the most part with the one and only Liberator we have. And it seems that still today the Word by which the world was formed has fallen silent. More likely, people have just stopped listening. Doctrines are shaped by cultural influences instead of the other way around. Along came Covid and emptied the churches; today we open the steeple and can scarcely find any people.

What do we do? And what do Christians do in a world that does not want to hear the good news? Like taking your car into the mechanic to get routine maintenance done, like calling someone to check your furnace or air conditioning at various times of the year, there are things we can do to restore our hope. But they entail engagement, not just thought or reflection.

9. Miller, *Disappearance of God*, 8.

10. Lewis, *Abolition of Man*, 35. Throughout his fiction and his apologetics, Lewis devotes regular attention to human longing for a better place where we will be fully known and fully ourselves. In *Till We Have Faces* the theme is repeated frequently as Psyche has longed since childhood to reach the mountain of her dreams, "To find the place where all the beauty came from. . . . Do you think it all meant nothing, all the longing? The longing for home?" (75–76).

They cost nothing less than your whole life. And they require exercise. Just as there is no point in getting your car tuned up if you only park it in the garage, and just as there is no point in getting your furnace overhauled if you never use it, hope is pointless unless you know what it is for and you use it. Let me suggest some steps that just might help us revive a bewildered hope.

The first step is to join a church rich in Bible study, orthodox in doctrine, and communal in fellowship. While Christianity emphasizes the personal relationship with Jesus Christ, and asserts that salvation arises out of that one-to-one relationship, it also believes in the strength and necessity of the community. Joining a church provides that. It testifies to the world that this is where I belong, this is where I stake my meaning.

It is true that church membership has fallen during the last decade. It is now lower than pre-pandemic days. But that is not surprising. More insidious is the multiplicity of cultural pressures that have challenged, and sometimes emptied, churches. We live in an era of splits and divisions and many people leave with no good place to go. Unless you are disabled, as I am, worshiping from home with a live service on a computer is nothing like being in the presence of believers for worship. The church provides fellowship, biblical and spiritual knowledge, the sacraments, and service. It is the key necessity in the survival of our hope.

The second step toward hope calls for a renewal of discernment. In this case I have in mind particularly the work of Satan to destroy our fellowship and churches and hope. In his moving "Templeton Address," Aleksandr Solzhenitsyn began by proclaiming a Russian adage: "Men have forgotten God; that's why all this has happened." If contemporaries have forgotten God, they have also forgotten the work and power of Satan. Satan's role in disturbing and destroying human affairs, particularly religious affairs, is everywhere affirmed in Scripture. Solzhenitsyn added, "It is here [in the people] that we see the dawn of hope: for no matter how formidably Communism bristles with tanks and rockets, no matter what successes it attains in seizing the planet, it is doomed never to vanquish Christianity."[11]

Although this second suggestion advocates a keen awareness of the work of Satan to disrupt and destroy the kingdom of God, this is not to the point of obsessiveness. In fact, one should be warned against that danger. God has allowed Satan a certain leeway on this earth: "Your enemy the devil prowls around like a roaring lion looking for someone to devour" (1 Pet 5:8). But the Bible also says in Romans 16:20: "The God of Peace will soon crush

11. Solzhenitsyn, "Templeton Address," 388.

Satan under your feet." Clearly, God sets the limits for Satan's prowling until such time as he will destroy Satan forever. In the meantime, God has left us weapons to thwart Satan's work: prayer, the Word of God, and the whole armor of God from Ephesians 6. What I am concerned about here is that really dangerous and foolish thing of ignoring Satan's work altogether.

The third suggestion is to what I call kingdom reading. First and foremost is reading regularly and devotionally from both the Old and New Testaments. In time the words seep into you; they become a part of your essential being. Bible reading is hard at first. So one starts with easier passages: one of the Gospels—Matthew, Mark, Luke, or John—and perhaps the book of Psalms. Then one moves to Isaiah and maybe Romans, with the ultimate aim of reading the Bible through cover to cover. If you have never done this, now is a good time to start. The key to kingdom reading is *regular* and *immersive* reading. From this start one can move to wider reading in addition. As Paul said: "We take captive every thought to make it obedient to Christ" (2 Cor 10:5). Each one of these steps makes the kingdom of God a little fuller and makes our hope a little clearer.

Let me summarize some characteristics of hope established thus far. All hope, but perhaps Christian hope especially, is something more than mere expectation. Hope is deep; it is profound, not frivolous. Hope doesn't originate so much in the mind, as it does someplace more visceral and primitive—what we may call the heart and soul. The warrant for that truth derives from 2 Corinthians 1:21: "Now it is God who makes both us and you stand firm in Christ. He anointed us, set his seal of ownership on us, and put his spirit in our hearts as a deposit, guaranteeing what is to come." Hope is imbued by the Holy Spirit on our souls.

Hope therefore is a yearning for something not yet wholly known, a longing for satisfaction of our deepest selves by some other agent who, we believe, loves us deeply. Hope is relational, not a wish. In Romans 8:24 Paul has been writing about Jesus's resurrection and our hope to be with him: "For in this hope we were saved. But hope that is seen is no hope at all. Who hopes for what he already has? But if we hope for what we do not yet have, we wait for it patiently." That hope is none other than union with our redeemer. This is a massive hope, one that takes all the years that the redeemer gives you to grow into it. After describing this present world as a place of "false hopes, dubious hopes, little hopes," Cornelius Plantinga Jr. argues that "Christian hope lodged in our Lord and his salvation is said with a resolute voice and written in capital letters across the New Testament. . . . Biblical hope is large, aggressive, confident."[12]

Finally, Christian hope grants the one thing that modern people are desperately searching for—the infinite and eternal value of the self. There is no such thing as a corporate salvation in Christianity. You won't be saved because you give a lot of money to worthy causes, nor because you were born into a right and proper family, or because you get driven to school in a limousine. Nor will you be saved because you panhandle on the street corner, or go to an inner-city church, or do forty-nine hours of community service each week. Salvation is all about you, all alone, before the Lord of the universe who somehow, through a miracle made new every day, looks you in the eye and loves you more than anyone who has ever lived. And he gives to you not the self you may have dreamed about, nor the self you have invented for Facebook or TikTok, but the self you really are because he designed it for you alone.

That is our deepest hope. The wonder of it is that our hope, finally, is not abstracted yearning after all. God has created you in his image. He has known you forever and will know you forever. Your name is graven on his palm. It is impossible for God to forget you. One thing God cannot do is stop his love for you. God's love establishes the goal of our hope, life everlasting in the perfect body he has waiting for you. In him all our hopes are yes and Amen.

12. Plantinga Jr., *Beyond Doubt*, 221.

Chapter Seven

An Issue of Trust

THE PARADOX OF TRUST is that we are aware of it least when we need it the most. I'm speaking about those days before the evil days draw near, as Ecclesiastes 12:1 has it. Before the evil days, when we were very young in body and soul, we depended on others for nearly everything. And others usually provided for us in such a warm, customary way that we took it for granted. We were secure; trust was kept. Trust in those days belonged to a Sunday school song: "Trust and obey, for there's no other way to be happy in Jesus, but to trust and obey." It was a pretty good Sunday school song, biblical to the core and free of higher criticism.

A few years later all children in my boyhood church were obligated to attend midweek catechism classes. As a tried and convicted ADHD youth, I managed to fail each memorization quiz in truly dramatic fashion. Midweek catechism was torture. Yet, I did manage to remember one, and only one, verse from those nerve-wracking years. It was the classic Proverbs 3:5–6: "Trust in the Lord with all your heart and lean not on your own understanding; in all your ways acknowledge him, and he will make your paths straight." Although I have never been a lover of straight paths, much preferring the crooked and undulating, somehow those words stuck with me.

Suffice it to say that trust was not an issue in my juvenile life. Or perhaps I should say, thoughts about trust or knowledge about it were absent. I can't recall my parents ever talking about trust. I can't remember ever having heard a sermon on trust, but neither have I ever heard a sermon on hell. I trusted that there was a heaven where all good little boys and girls would go, and I may have heard now and then that some particularly bad person was going "straight to hell." To my callow mind, that was probably the equivalent of having to go to the grocery store. Hell held no horrors because we never heard of any. Trust was firm because we had not yet experienced the heartache of broken trust.

The odd thing, when I pause to reflect on trust, is that I have lived a life of trust, even if having been, for the most part, unaware of it. Like most people's, my youth passed largely unperturbed by issues of trust. Many people, I imagine, will point to close friends or a good marriage as evidence of trust. I have been blessed with both, but that isn't quite what I mean. I mean, for one thing, those moments when you just give yourself to a task without really understanding the risks. You *assume* everything will be all right. Here's an example. For a while, right at the start of my teaching career, I did house painting in the summer to pay the leftover bills that my beginner's salary could not quite touch. I believe I would have done it anyway for the sheer joy of spending a summer outdoors with three of my best friends, the radio blaring golden oldies, the sun warm, the house transforming into a thing of beauty.

The only problem was that one of the crew was afraid of heights, so I and my friend Andy had to do all the high-ladder work on the thirty-six-foot and forty-foot ladders. That's a long way up there, especially the house in Slippery Rock, Pennsylvania, that had a 100-foot sheer cliff at the back. It fell away literally fifteen feet from the back of the house. One of the bottom-story painters had a talent for securing the ladders on tricky projects, digging the feet in the soil, using four-foot crow bars to brace them in the ground. Only when he was done was I ready to swing my leg out over the cliff, catch the ladder step, and climb my way to the third story peak. I trusted the forty-foot, aluminum ladder, after my partner had secured it.

Trust is most often like that, I realize. You act on a condition, but with the certainty that someone has secured it. You assume that something—a pinned-down ladder, a favorite car, a close friend—will behave in its tried-and-true pattern. You may be said to trust it. Trust is based on someone or something with proven dependability; then you commit yourself fully to the conditions. I climb the ladder. I drive the car. I go out for lunch with my friend.

But even as I settled on that definition, more influenced by ladders than any theological concept of the word, I grew aware of how very little I actually understood about trust. Something about trust defies neat and easy definition. Glandion Carney and William Long, in their *Trusting God Again*, observe that "Trust is very fragile, as fragile and brittle as a clay pot in [a] bone-dry state. Trust is like an exotic and sensitive flowering plant that flourishes only under optimal conditions but tends to fade, wither and die when struck by severe adversity."[1] Yet we hold that trust is a virtue. We want it in our lives. We want to be able to trust others.

For various reasons we find it difficult. As I look for neat, crisp definitions, and find instead stories of hurt and dismay, I realize that trust is something that lies deep in the soul. It shades the very essence of who we are and who we want to be. We want to be trustworthy; we want to trust others. That is why, quite simply, broken trust rives a person to the very soul.

Defining trust begins at a level of believing that someone is dependable. He or she, like the ladder, the car, the good friend, has been tested and proven. That person acts in the present as she has acted in the past and as we trust that she will in the future. Very close to dependability, secondly, is predictability. Given certain circumstances, we can say that this will be the response of a person we trust. For example, if we confess our sins to God, and ask to be forgiven, then according to all that we know about God we can be assured that he will forgive us. We even have his ironclad agreement in Scripture that he will forgive our sins. In 1 John 1:9 we find: "If we confess our sins, he is faithful and just and will forgive us our sins and purify us from all unrighteousness." Moreover, John points out in the very next chapter that Jesus actively intercedes for us with the Father: "But if anybody does sin, we have one who speaks to the Father in our defense—Jesus Christ, the Righteous One" (2:1).

So, we have pretty good evidence that we can trust Jesus. Being God, by definition being absolute, God himself is the absolute authority for what he says. If he wasn't, he wouldn't be God. And in multiple places God tells us that we can trust him. What we don't have is a God who will come down by our chairside, listen to us, and grant whatever we wish. Jesus isn't a genie in a green bottle. Above all else, Jesus is just. He is true to his revealed nature. We can trust that he will treat us in perfect justice—that is, restore us sinners to a right relationship with him through the power of

1. Carney and Long, *Trusting God Again*, 22.

forgiveness and the cross. But he will always behave in perfect justice; that is precisely why we can trust him.

A telling example of trust in God appears in the first chapters of Deuteronomy, as the Israelites, fearful and ornery as ever, balk at crossing into the promised land. Moses has to pass the torch of leadership to the younger generation and give some final directions to the people before they enter that promised land. That is a journey the Israelites don't care to undertake. In Deuteronomy 1:28, the people protest: "Where can we go? Our brothers have made us lose heart. They say, 'The people are stronger and taller than we are; the cities are large, with walls up to the sky. We even saw the Anakites there.'" Moses reassures them by recalling God's steadfast leadership and protection in the past. "In spite of this," he adds, "you did not trust in the Lord your God, who went ahead of you on your journey, in fire by night and in a cloud by day, to search out places for you to camp and to show you the way you should go" (Deut 1:34–36). The passage significantly informs us of just why we can and should trust God. He has already demonstrated his loving care for us. Our tendency, however, when we scan the past of our own lives, is either to take our blessings for granted, or to believe we have them as a consequence of our own labor, cunning, or power.

Trust is built as we review and consider the way another person or God himself has treated us through the past. That is why Moses spends the next few chapters of Deuteronomy recalling the many times God stepped directly into Israelite history to deliver them. "What other nation is so great as to have their gods near them the way the Lord our God is near us whenever we pray to him?" (Deut 4:7). Moreover, Moses promises that God will continue to be with his people: "But if from there you seek the Lord your God, you will find him if you look for him with all your heart and with all your soul" (Deut 4:29). And finally, "You were shown these things so that you might know that the Lord is God; besides him there is no other" (Deut 4:35).

Moses summons the evidence here at a crucial juncture. The promised land comes with a load of terrors, from giants (including a king who slept in a thirteen-foot bed) to roaming tribes set upon their demise. These Israelites were not the hardened warriors who with Saul and David and Solomon settled a kingdom in the later days. These were nomads who ate from God's menu quail and manna and drank water from a rock. They didn't even know how to provide for themselves. It's no wonder their feet shook in their sandals. Moses has to buoy their trust in God, and he does it by reminding them of how God had taken care of them in the past.

The second thing Moses does in his task of cementing the people's trust in God is to remind them of the customs and commands that kept them in a vital relationship with God. Trust is a two-way street. If it's hard to trust someone when you have no record of their character; it is also hard when there are no defining guidelines for your relationship. Therefore, Moses recollects for the people the history of God's dealings with them.

Moses's methods hold sway over much of the Old Testament as various leaders address the people's fears. Often, they turned to God as the one, wholly trustworthy being. In Psalm 49:5–9 we read: "Why should I fear when evil days come, when wicked deceivers surround me—those who trust in their wealth and boast of their great riches? No man can redeem the life of another or give to God a ransom for him—the ransom for a life is costly, no payment is ever enough—that he should live on forever and not see decay." Here the words clearly point to the New Testament and Jesus as the perfect sacrifice. Such declarations as this in Psalm 56:11, "In God I trust; I will not be afraid" are frequent. Furthermore, we have the emphatic words of Jesus in John 14:1: "Do not let your hearts be troubled. Trust in God; trust also in me." Following that appears the "many rooms" passage where Jesus promises an eternal home for believers.

The Bible, then, holds that God is dependable, predictable, and just—all strong grounds for trusting him. Nonetheless, we moderns find it almost hopelessly difficult to trust. Especially our fellow humans. Surrounded by the darkness of sordid events that plague our present age, and the ruthless violation of trust at all levels, we find very good reasons to guard our trust. In fact, an age of damaged trust turns us inward. We adapt a carapace as hard as steel to keep others from entering our private lives. While the action of trust is always outward, toward another being, broken trust turns inward to a world of self-reliance.

Consider the fact that trust is an action, one whereby we place our faith, our *fides*, our trust in someone else. We expose ourselves to that person. We give up intimacy and dependence. The opposite action, logically, is not to trust no one, but to trust only oneself. We hide intimacy deep within; we depend only on ourselves. We trust only ourselves. T. S. Eliot drew a powerful image of this rage for self-sufficiency in his poem *The Waste Land*.[2] The sound of *Dayadhvam* rumbles as thunder in the

2. Eliot, "Waste Land," *Collected Poems*, See II.412–15.

distance, forming in the narrator's mind the Sanskrit word that translates as *sympathize*. Eliot ponders what it means to sympathize in this modern age. A picture comes to his mind of us moderns pulling a prison door shut on ourselves, reaching through the bars for the key, withdrawing it and locking ourselves inside. We live in our self-made prisons, without sympathy, without trust. In his classic study *Knowing God*, J. I. Packer describes the imprisoned self: "Christian minds have been conformed to the modern spirit: the spirit, that is, that spawns great thoughts of man and leaves room for only small thoughts of God. The modern way with God is to set him at a distance."[3]

We have seen that we can trust another person when we find that person dependable, predictable, and just. These qualities are grounds for our trust. Moreover, we witnessed the imprimatur in both the Old and New Testaments to trust God. Yet even these do not seem to express the full dynamics of trust. It might be helpful to think for a few minutes about some of those qualities that stand opposed to trust. It is, after all, a time-tested method for understanding virtues generally. We might ask, for example, which virtue stands opposite the vice of pride? We can answer that humility is juxtaposed to pride, just as chastity is juxtaposed to lust, and diligence is juxtaposed to sloth.

The antonym of trust, or its opposing vice, would be the thing or activity that blocks the good thing of trust. Psychologically speaking, we could answer that suspicion is the thing that blocks trust. There are people born with a suspicious mind. They hunt for ulterior motives. They refuse to take people and statements at face value. They believe in hidden meanings. Such a mind, however it is formed, is instinctively slow to trust. We do have to grant that many people, bruised along life's way, have a good reason to be suspicious. Sometimes suspicion is another word for wisdom. But the moral antonym of trust, we find to be greed.

While trust always opens yourself before another person—the person you trust—greed always turns to someone else to see what can be taken from them. Trust honors a self; greed takes from a self. Greed uses others—the opposite of trust. In her study of the vices, Rebecca DeYoung writes: "Greed can captivate the young, the old, and everyone in between. In all its varied expressions of gain and grasping, however, greed is a perverted love. Its profile has disordered desire written all over it."[4]

3. Packer, *Knowing God*, 6.

4. DeYoung, *Glittering Vices*, 113.

It is little wonder that Scripture has much to say by way of condemning greed. In Isaiah 57:17 God says, "I was enraged by his sinful greed; I punished him and hid my face in anger." And in Romans 1 we find the infamous "God gave them over" catalogue, where humanity turns away from God to pursue their sins and God thereby gives them over to their sins. In verses 28–29 we read: "Since they did not think it worthwhile to retain the knowledge of God, he gave them over to a depraved mind, to do what ought not to be done. They have become filled with every kind of wickedness, evil, greed and depravity."

Colossians 2:5 provides an interesting twist in the list of sins in which the wayward indulge: "Put to death, therefore, whatever belongs to your earthly nature: sexual immorality, impurity, lust, evil desires and greed, which is idolatry." The twist lies in calling greed idolatry, where the obsessive pursuit of wealth and material goods take the place of devotion to God. Greed, like the sexual obsessions listed in the verse, subsumes one's whole being. While trying to fill oneself with material possessions, one discovers that there is no longer any room for God himself. Greed is therefore idolatry.

Greed is one of the more common idols of our age; yet, there is really nothing new about greed. In Habakkuk 2:5 God responds to the prophet's concerns about the Babylonians: "He [the Babylonian] is arrogant and never at rest. Because he is as greedy as the grave and like death is never satisfied, he gathers to himself all the nations and takes captive all the peoples." Such people still run wild over God's word and human lives today. Timothy Keller is quite accurate when he observes that "According to the Bible, idolaters do three things with their idols. They love them, trust them, and obey them."[5] So deeply engrained do these idols become, writes Keller, that "We begin to realize that idols cannot simply be removed. They must be replaced. If you only try to uproot them, they grow back; but they can be supplanted. By what? By God himself, of course."[6]

The disease that destroys trust, then, begins with the self-sufficiency and self-gratification that lock the patient inward. If we continue the analogy of a deadly disease, we see that those symptoms also deepen into a demanding greed to satisfy the self. At this stage the deadly qualities become the only important things in the patient's life. In effect, they harden into idolatry as they possess the patient utterly. The situation is critical,

5. Keller, *Counterfeit Gods*, 56–57.

6. Keller, *Counterfeit Gods*, 155.

demanding a complete idolectomy. The good news is that the surgery is free, even if acute pain is undergone in the process. It hurts to give up idols. So much so that the only balm is the grace of forgiveness.

A large part of sustaining trust, in fact, lies in the art of giving and receiving forgiveness. Not only before God, but also before our fellows, we need to grow adept at forgiving. Certain people are not interested in forgiveness, nor in trust. We all know people very much like those described here: self-imprisoning, self-gratifying, avaricious for possessions and ever greedy for more. Such are only capable of trusting themselves; they refuse to give themselves up for another. Their idols seem unshakable, girded by shiny possessions and bloated investments. Trusting another, even trusting God, threatens these things. When one comes to trust God fully, one realizes that all these shiny baubles come from God in the first place. We are temporary caretakers, finding ways to give them back to God.

It is interesting to ponder that in heaven trust will no longer be an issue. Trust will not be able to be broken. Unfortunately, on this earth it gets broken all the time. Trust is very fragile; it breaks easily and causes ruptures in the heart. Forgiveness helps. The passage of time to re-establish trust is essential. Yet it is also essential and healing to trust again. The final healing comes from God. Psalm 147:3–4 has it like this: "[The Lord] heals the brokenhearted and binds up their wounds. Great is our Lord and mighty in power; his understanding has no limit." With a healing and understanding God like that, trust at all levels is worth the infinite risk.

Chapter Eight

Integrity

In the Corner Glass Office

NO MATTER HOW MANY times we have done this before, each time seems like the first time. Anxiety rides in the back seat. Rough, booted heels kick the front seat, reminding us of its presence.

It is a pretty drive, tunneling through a variety of trees that grow to the edge of the road. Streams cut their courses around hills and valleys. Some things, like this ride and like this visit, I just don't get used to. Unable to drive because of my disability, I own the shotgun seat and can take in the view. To this day, I don't think I can tell you a single thing about that drive, not the name of one park, not the name of a single store. Like America's anthem of the 1970s, "There were plants and birds and rocks and things."[1] But anxiety and anticipation were too big in the car to let things in.

The car dips into a long, wooded valley. We turn into the long uphill gap where we can see the towers looming on each side of the highway. Then the sun breaks apart on coils of razor wire, exploding in light like Christmas decorations. For some reason, we park in the same spot every time, although there is plenty of room to park elsewhere. I think it may be a small psychological trick to impose something routine, something certain on a place that couldn't be more uncertain.

1. America, "A Horse with No Name," by Dewey Bunnell. *America* (Warner Records), 1971.

Odd, that the state built two of these monstrosities, one on each side of the road. They stand, red-bricked and massive, snarling at each other through barbwire teeth. All day, all year long.

Inside the front door a prisoner is buffing the lobby floor. He also does this all day long, erasing the signs of heavy traffic as soon as they appear. The futility of it all brings an ache in my heart. He smiles and nods as we walk past. We always greet him happily, complimenting the shiny floor. He nods again, head bobbing on a thin neck ribbed with ligaments and tendons like a stalk of rhubarb. Then I notice he has plugs in his ears.

We stop at the desk, exchange identifications and other information. My wife does this. I'm trying to balance with the help of my cane. I wouldn't want to fall over on the clean floor. Everything here moves in slow motion. At least in prison you can touch the prisoner; in jail almost all visitation is now remote, over closed-circuit televisions. Once the exchange is completed, we turn to the waiting area. It is busy today; almost thirty people are angled into the hard folding chairs. And we wait.

Heads turn when a young woman is told she will have to "cover up." Her blouse has a low-cut, scooped neck. A store a mile down the road stocks shelves of prim shirts and sweaters that button to the neck, thoroughly hiding any hint of cleavage. We wait.

Some people exit through the sally port with locking gates at either end. The same number of people enter it to be frisked, x-rayed, mouths searched, shoes and socks taken off so the toes can be searched. A guard works over my wooden cane every single time. It's oak; solid oak. For all his relentless effort, it will not come apart. We pass muster and line up by the gate that leads to a gray hallway. The huddle of anxious people begins to smell. There are always a few unwashed bodies flavoring the crowd. Heat pumps through ceiling vents.

Visitors retrieve their plastic baggies jammed with quarters for the vending machines and exit the sally port into a narrow gray corridor. Another prisoner stands bent and worn behind a buffing machine, waiting for the crowd to disperse. Another checkpoint, and then we are reunited with our loved one. Still loved desperately despite these dank, ceremonial walls.

Then, the visit ends at its allotted time. The quarters are all spent in the vending machines: a lukewarm cheeseburger, fire hot Doritos, an assortment of candy and drinks. We enter the sally port. While standing there, waiting for the second gate to unlock, trying to catch a puff of fresher air, I overhear the guard say to someone else in line, someone who had complimented the procedure, "Yes. This prison has integrity."

And I was left with something to ponder during the long ride back home.

What could a prison possibly have to do with integrity? In and of itself, *integrity* is a dauntingly hard word to define. Or perhaps it's more accurate to say that it answers to so many definitions and connotations. Integrity is often used to imply honesty, or at least one can say that people of integrity aren't liars. There's the faintest blush of sincerity about the word, but I'm not sure that anyone is really sure what sincerity means. Some terms, we realize, are difficult to define with precision. Meanings shade and shift under the pressure of time. Varied contexts influence understanding. Still, a prison having integrity? That's not easy to wrap your mind around.

One common understanding of integrity has to do with living according to ethical values. Maybe that can be applied to a prison in that the staff attempts to treat the prisoners as if they were ethically valuable. That, unfortunately, is a regrettably naïve view of prison life. Prison is a living nightmare. And even though some prisoners can put their best face forward for an hour or so to attend a class or a visit, that time is brief. No one in prison is named Pollyanna. I think then that the guard may have had something in mind like orderly or well-governed by the term *integrity.*

* * * * *

Nonetheless, integrity appears to have a large and important role in modern life. It is esteemed as a virtue, although no doubt a lesser cousin of the Divine Triad. Integrity is something we want to be known for, even if we don't know for certain what it is. We should push this effort to define it a bit further to see what we can find, or to see if integrity is indeed worth seeking out.[2] As I researched the term further, I made an interesting discovery. In

2. It is difficult to isolate and define the multivarious meanings of integrity. While standing before a powerful landscape painting, we might say that it has integrity. In this case we speak of a certain unity in the artwork, a sense that all the parts are in harmony, that the work has an appropriate fittingness. Indeed, we could say the same about the landscape in its physical reality. We might even say that there is virtue inherent in the painting or the landscape because of its integrity. But this kind of aesthetic reference can get very tricky. For example, one might say that Jackson Pollock's *The Moon Woman*, hanging in the Guggenheim, has integrity even though the composition consists of weird body parts and dislocated angles that are intellectually disharmonious. Instead, the harmony arises through color and line.

our present age, it seems that integrity has become the province of business and other corporate leadership positions. A raft of books has been floated on "Principles for Leadership" and the like. In business, integrity earns a high rank. What follows is a brief sampling of the many book titles for business leaders that have appeared in the last few years:

- *Leading for Impact: The CEO's Guide to Influencing with Integrity (2024)*
- *Integrity: The Courage to Meet the Demands of Reality (2009)*
- *Selling Ethically: A Business Parable Connecting Integrity with Profits (2020)*
- *Integrity-Integrity: In Times Like These (2009)*
- *The Ethical Sellout: Maintaining Your Integrity in the Age of Compromise (2019)*

I live in the mid-sized city of Grand Rapids, Michigan. It's a fine city to dwell in, to live and move in and have your being. It is also a mecca for small or medium-sized businesses, especially if those businesses practice integrity. In fact, Grand Rapids has a whole slew of businesses named for integrity. A quick glance shows Integrity Business Solutions, Integrity Financial Group, Integrity Tax Group, Integrity Educational Services, Integrity RV Parts, Integrity Handyman Services, and perhaps another half- dozen Integrities.

Just what do all these businesses mean by it? I suppose at the crassest level integrity is used to bestow a touch of class. It's like the word *imperial* of my youth. It designated everything from oil for your car, to butter in your refrigerator, to the cigar your father smoked in the evening. Purportedly, imperial products were bigger and better, of royal bearing, the cat's meow. So too with integrity: this is a special business, set off from all those lesser, non-integrity businesses.

Maybe. Then again, maybe the business owners just like the feel, the appeal, of the name Integrity. They want to convey the idea that this is an honest, square-dealing, dependable business. In fact, I had the pleasure of speaking with the president and owner of one such business, and in his case at least the name Integrity was specifically and carefully chosen. Over the course of several decades this owner—I'll call him Robert—grew a very successful business that even expanded to several locations. The deal that a competing conglomerate offered him seemed like a sweetheart deal. They would buy his company and pay him to stay on to run it.

Except they wanted Robert to run it according to the conglomerate's rules. They knew only one rule—profit. Nothing else mattered. Not the employees; not the customers. Just profit. When Robert took issue with some of their orders, they fired him. In modern business it is not unheard of to be fired from the company you yourself founded. It just does not show much integrity.

Never one to dwell on losses, Robert started another company according to his values. This company would function according to integrity: looking out for the customer, having a deep concern for employees and their needs, paying bills on time, and dozens of other qualities that honored the word *Integrity* in the new business title. Robert demonstrated that one can run a highly successful business and still pursue ethical values.

From prison to the business world, perhaps we can make some initial conclusions about the nature of integrity. Integrity, then, is a strong connection between what you believe and value and how you live. Like an excellent work of art, it is a matter of "fittingness." I live how I believe. I am not one person in church on Sunday morning and another at work on Monday afternoon. I am consistent in life and belief. That is step one of integrity.

* * * * *

It is a good first step, but there is more. For a long time now, I have been deeply attracted to a slim volume of essays by C. S. Lewis called *The Weight of Glory*. In the title essay Lewis writes:

> Do you think I am trying to weave a spell? Perhaps I am; but remember your fairy tales. Spells are used for breaking enchantments as well as for inducing them. And you and I have need of the strongest spell that can be found to wake us from the evil enchantment of worldliness which has been laid upon us for nearly a hundred years. Almost our whole education has been directed to silencing this shy, persistent, inner voice; almost all our modern philosophies have been devised to convince us that the good of man is to be found on this earth.[3]

There is a way of living other than worldliness. It is living in integrity, according to one's higher beliefs and values.

3. Lewis, *Weight of Glory*, 5.

If our first step toward understanding integrity is holding to a correspondence between beliefs and actions, then we must call for some qualifications. It is true that some people have thoroughly bad ethical beliefs—spitefully abusing others, for example, or treating people meanly—that should not be put into action. Their actions harm and offend others. People like that just don't care about what others think. They continue their abusive way in the world like bulldozers, obliterating everything in their path. Unfortunately, they also prowl our neighborhoods, our businesses, and our schools, and maybe the house next door. To them, integrity is a word that tastes like ashes on the tongue, burned up and useless.

If we are going to make integrity meaningful and practical, then, it seems that we will have to qualify that connectedness between belief and actions. Fortunately, a very precise constellation of qualities orbit integrity that can enlighten us. Several distinct qualities in particular work together in syncretic fashion to form the whole of this important virtue.

First among these qualities is that living a life of integrity is living *an ordered life*. This is neither easily done nor commonly done. Our lives are intruded upon; unexpected events throw order into turmoil. Consequently, this modern generation longs for dependability. People want something to count on, something they can know for sure, something with integrity. Instead, life seems too often random and veering out of control.

In their 1968 *White Album*, the Beatles heralded the song of the age: "Helter Skelter."

The chorus echoes the dizzying, discordant mood:

> When I get to the bottom I go back to the top of the slide
> Where I stop and I turn and I go for a ride
> Till I get to the bottom and I see you again
> Yeah yeah yeah hey.[4]

It spoke to an age in random circularity, in which no order may be found. We might also remember that "Helter Skelter" became the theme song of the murderous Charles Manson clan as they wreaked random havoc up the California coast. Upon such brutal discord, integrity attempts to redeem the age by imposing order.

An orderly world, secondly, is a *whole* world. By that I mean a certain fittingness is at work. There is a clear designation of responsibilities. The business-place model we considered earlier is apropos here too. A business

4. The Beatles, "Helter Skelter," *The White Album* (1968).

that seeks integrity will have a clear designation of authority and responsibilities. Everyone, from leaders to employees, will have clearly defined tasks. They will also not intrude upon the tasks of others. Although we would all grant that at a company practicing integrity each person has a voice that must be heard, each voice also has its own area of expertise or province of responsibility. While I might be a very skilled forklift driver, I would be a complete failure as the chief financial officer.

While the business world serves as a good model for order according to fitting talents or gifts, the model is applicable to many institutions. A family, for example, can function more orderly when there is a clear designation of responsibilities. So too does a church, a school, or countless organizations that work best when they work with integrity. In her study *The Way of Integrity*, Martha Beck observes that "The word *integrity* has taken on a slightly prim, judgmental nuance in modern English, but the word comes from the Latin *integer*, which simply means 'intact.' To be in integrity is to be one thing, whole and undivided. When a plane is in integrity, all its millions of parts work together smoothly and cooperatively. If it loses integrity, it may stall, falter, or crash. There's no judgment here. Just physics."[5] We can apply Beck's observations to any organization made up of multiple units: Integrity may be achieved only when the disparate parts are ordered into a working whole. They also apply to the individual who subjects her differing interests and activities in one unified purpose for living,

Third, the ordered life or the ordered community (business, church, school, government, and so forth) achieves integrity when it is honest. *Honest* is not a particularly difficult or complex word. In both etymology and derivations, it has always meant pretty much the same thing. It's one of those words that "means what it says." And what it says is that honest people are free from fabrication or lying. They are truth-tellers. In fact, in many sources honesty is listed as a synonym for integrity. While I would hesitate to see them as identical, clearly honesty or truth-telling is a necessary constituent of integrity.

That honesty or truth-telling, and those two do seem to be synonyms, receives biblical mandate hardly needs mention. They are essential to Christian faith. And that lying, or falsification, is considered heinous and a threat

5. Beck, *Way of Integrity*, xiv. See also Chuck Chapman, who states: "The word *integrity* and the word *integration* are both derived from the Latin *integrare*, meaning 'whole or unbroken.' *Integration* means bringing several things together to form a whole, and *integrity* means the whole is working together to produce an outcome." *Finding Your Way Without Losing Yourself*, 11.

to truth hardly needs mention either. We might ask, however, just why these contrary values are so frequently repeated and emphasized in Scripture. It all hangs on the fact that Jesus is the source of truth. The apostle John put it like this: "We have seen his glory, the glory of the One and Only, who came from the Father, full of grace and truth" (John 1:14).

As Jesus's preaching is recorded in the Gospels, he prefaces many of his commentaries with the words, "I tell you the truth." Repeatedly, Jesus proclaims himself as the truth-teller. In fact, when standing before Pilate, Jesus says, "For this reason I was born and for this I came into the world, to testify to the truth" (John 18:37).

Honesty and truth have been the subjects of music from the oldest hymns to modern rock. Most people are familiar with Martin Luther's classic hymn "A Mighty Fortress Is Our God." The third verse heralds the timeless struggle between evil and truth:

> And though this world, with devils filled,
> Should threaten to undo us,
> We will not fear, for God has willed
> His truth to triumph through us.[6]

In the modern era, Billy Joel released his song "Honesty" in 1979, and Beyoncé covered it in 2008, singing that honesty "is such a lonely word." Billy Joel is unapologetic in his assessment of the age, claiming that everyone is untrue.[7] The two songs leave us at a crossroad: Will God's truth triumph through us? Or, do we live hopelessly and captively in a world of duplicity and falsehood?

Thus far we have noted three essential qualities for living in integrity. It requires living in an ordered world, living in a whole or unified manner, and living honestly as a truth-teller. The final quality of living in integrity is living justly. Immediately red flags start flying. Just, justice, justly—is there a page of Scripture that doesn't overtly or suggestively deal with them? When John writes the following at the end of his Gospel, "Jesus did many other things as well. If every one of them were written down, I suppose that even the whole world would not have room for the books that would be written" (21:25), he may have been thinking just about those books on justice. Yet, to see the crucial link between integrity and justice, the scope may be narrowed considerably.

6. Luther, "Mighty Fortress," 444.

7. Billy Joel, "Honesty," *52nd Street* (1978).

As a preliminary matter, it is beneficial to sample just two or three of those references in Scripture. After all, we do assume that the Bible is the basis for living in integrity, and in matters of justice it is wonderfully practical. Its descriptions of justice form life lessons. For example, Deuteronomy 16 has a passage about appointing judges, and Moses states: "Do not accept a bribe, for a bribe blinds the eyes of the wise and twists the words of the righteous. Follow justice and justice alone, so that you may live and possess the land the Lord your God is giving you" (19–20). Here we see a very applicable quality of integrity: Refuse bribes of any kind; instead live by justice.

As Scripture refers to the theme of justice, the objects of justice grow clear. Biblical justice is particularly aimed at the poor, at women, and at children. The prophet Amos addresses the Israelites on this score. First comes the indictment against the nation: "You trample on the poor and force him to give you grain. Therefore, though you have built stone mansions, you will not live in them" (5:11). He returns to his indictment a few lines following: "You oppress the righteous and take bribes and you deprive the poor of justice in the courts" (5:12). Then Amos sees the judgment day of the Lord coming. He encourages us in the meantime to "Let justice roll on like a river, righteousness like a never-failing stream" (5:24).

Biblical justice is directed toward the disadvantaged. It sounds a militant call to count those who don't count in society. Why is this? To answer, travel back to the beginning. In Genesis 1:27 we find that "God created man in his own image, in the image of God he created him; male and female he created them." However dissolute or disheveled, that panhandler on the corner is an image-bearer of Christ. Justice insists that that person has rights—to be clothed, to be fed, to be cared for. In his book *Journey Toward Justice*, Nicholas Wolterstorff writes, "My own view is that rights are grounded in the worth, the value, the dignity of human beings. We all have worth on account of some achievement on our part, some capacity that we possess, some property that we have, some relationship in which we stand."[8] I appreciate that strong sense of human worth, but perhaps it can be made even more specific to fulfill the biblical mandate to justice. In this case, people have rights because they are image-bearers of God. They have rights even if they are not capable of achieving anything; they have rights even if they have no property; they have rights if they have no relationships but live in lonely isolation. They have rights if they

8. Wolterstorff, *Journey Toward Justice*, 47.

are disabled and capable of far less than they wish. They have rights if they suffer from lack of medicines that might grant some mental stability. They have rights if they are fetuses or 103 years old. Justice won't stand for the privileged rights. We need a larger frame.

We find that in the relationship between justice and justification. In Luke 18 we find Jesus's parable of the persistent widow. As he so often did, Jesus reflects on the story he has just told, making certain that the disciples catch the different meanings that emerge. After setting aside the judge in the story as "unjust," Jesus adds: "And will God bring about justice for his chosen ones, who cry out to him day and night? Will he keep putting them off? I tell you, he will see that they get justice, and quickly" (7–8). Actually, God's justice comes in two phases: one already accomplished and with us in the death and resurrection of Jesus; the other yet to come in the final judgment.

Jesus's incarnation, the life he lived, and the death he died, were acts of justice in which he paid the demands of sin and the agony of iniquity in our stead. Isaiah wrote "My righteous servant will justify many" (53:11). Isaiah continues his justification discourse in verse 12, a verse echoed by Paul in his great exposition of justice and justification in Romans. While examining what it means to have righteousness credited to us, Paul writes: "The words 'It was credited to him' were written not for him alone, but also for us, to whom God will credit righteousness—for us who believe in him who raised Jesus our Lord from the dead. He was delivered over to death for our sins and was raised for our justification" (4:23–25).

Justification is one of the central rocks on which the Christian life is founded. Paul summarizes in Romans 5:9: "Since we have now been justified by his blood, how much more shall we be saved from God's wrath through him!" But there is always a question following the statement of belief in Christian doctrine: How now shall we live? Here the implication turns full circle. We began by considering the nature of justice and also the biblical mandate to doing justice. This duty to meet human needs and to honor human rights flows directly from God's imperative. It becomes a sacred duty as we are mindful of the grace of justification, where God met our most dire need with the death and resurrection of his Son.

An interesting statement appears as Paul begins to wrap up his discourse in chapter 8. He writes: Those [God] called, he also justified; those he justified, he also glorified" (30). If we are justified, we are also *called*. That is, we are called to do something, not simply to rest in spiritual comfort.

If justified, one thing we are called to do is to behave justly. We are to do justice—actively, deliberately, unceasingly.

If we are wanting to live a life of integrity (and we *should* desire it and want it), then we do well to pursue these qualities of order, unity or fittingness of parts into a whole, honesty, and justice. All these are subsumed under the major effort to have a connectedness between values and actions. Integrity is often seen as an ideal, something we often strive toward but ultimately fall short of. That attitude seems to me to be wrong. Integrity is attainable. It may be an ideal, but it is one that finds its ultimate meaning when lived out in the daily hustle and grind.

Finally, a note of qualification is in order. It is very easy to get discouraged in the pursuit of integrity. Sometimes the person trying to act in integrity feels like a tiny island in the middle of a smarmy, polluted sea. Such a person may wonder if it's even worth the effort, given all the competitors who seem to be surging ahead on a super-slick surface of lies and dirty deals. I wonder if they are really getting ahead, or whether they are sinking into the cesspool of iniquity that marks so much of our contemporary world. It's better, I should think, to stand firm with integrity than sink with iniquity.

Chapter Nine

Wisdom and Her Books

WITH ALL THE DESCRIPTIONS of wisdom in the Bible, and the plethora of figures of speech surrounding her, questions still arise concerning just what wisdom is, where she is found, and what her purposes are. We can clear up one mystery quickly; wisdom is a *her*, modeled on the Greek female figure for justice named Sophia, a lady in good standing in the religious-philosophical community of the ancients, and adapted for Christian purposes.

Lady Wisdom[1] retains her femininity in the Bible, honored as she is in the Hebraic tradition. We commonly speak of three Wisdom Books in the Old Testament—Job, Proverbs, and Ecclesiastes. These three are foundational and all scholars agree to their inclusion as wisdom books. Some people add Psalms and Song of Solomon and call it five wisdom books. Some add a couple of books from the Apocrypha to stretch it to seven.

A very nice illustration found in Proverbs helps clarify the place and purpose of wisdom. The scene in Proverbs 9 is a residential district on a busy city thoroughfare. At one end of the block rests the house of Wisdom—neat, tidy, and inviting, everyone seems to know that it is there. In fact, Wisdom's house stands on seven strong pillars. It is not easily shaken. Here Wisdom prepares a bountiful feast, then sends out her maidens to invite others in. Wisdom herself stands at the highest point of the city, calling to the simple and ordinary to come in. Above all, she calls: "The

1. For the sake of convenience, in this chapter I will capitalize Wisdom when the name refers to the person. The use of lower-case signifies the common noun wisdom.

fear of the Lord is the beginning of wisdom, and knowledge of the Holy One is understanding" (Prov 9:10).

At the other end of the block squats the house of Folly. Since visitors come often to gratify their pleasures and have a good time, the house is ill-kempt and slovenly. We might picture it as an unpainted clapboard hovering over an alley. On the rickety front porch, raised a good distance above street level, sits the owner, Folly. She calls out, also to the simple and ordinary, enticing anyone to enter and indulge their secret desires. Many turn eagerly toward her, "But little do they know that the dead are there, that her guests are in the depths of the grave" (9:18). The final picture of Folly's house is nothing quite so much as a mausoleum, its interior stuffed with victims lying in their burial crypts and lost for all time.

Both voices call us today. We are positioned on that street, caught in the traffic with a choice to make. To understand the principles of that choice, we need to explore three things about wisdom: the source of wisdom, the purpose of wisdom, and the *imago Dei* as God's wisdom in us. But first, a few preliminary matters are in order.[2]

The Wisdom Books

We should understand that wisdom literature was common in the Old Testament era, flourishing through world civilizations that sought order and virtue for the state. Perhaps the earliest examples were from Egypt as early as 3000 years BC. In the Hebraic nation, wisdom became a personal and state concern around the time of the kings, or about 1000 years BC. The Orient had its wisdom literature too, generally dated to the life of Confucius in China from 531–479 BC. In all such circumstances, the theme of wisdom literature was to discern and relate certain teachings from wise individuals. The aim was to direct a virtuous life and to comprehend the ways of the world or the working of a divinity in the world.

2. Several helpful studies aid our understanding of the wisdom books. Robert Alter, *Wisdom Books*, provides a new translation of the books, along with a commentary. It has a helpful introduction. Daniel J. Estes, in *Message of Wisdom*, engages a biblical study of wisdom, examining the wisdom books in the place of Scripture as a whole. Finally, Herbert Lockyer wrote *7 Pillars of Wisdom*, a study based on Proverbs 9. The seven pillars, according to Lockyer, are Mystery, Incarnation, Vindication, Revelation, Proclamation, Belief, and Glorification. Unfortunately, the concept of hidden wisdom, like the first century Gnostics, has also spawned a flurry of self-help books with special instructions. Christian Kurch has self-published several of these books. His latest 2024 release is typically titled *How to Live Your Faith Becoming Rich*.

These teachings would then be formed into aphorisms or maxims and collected for distribution.

Although we are not certain how many writers were involved in the composition of Proverbs, the section titled "Proverbs of Solomon" with its two-line maxims filling chapters 10–21 most clearly typifies the historical pattern of wisdom literature. Here we find the compact statements that have so thoroughly entered the Western world that many attribute them to cultural wisdom rather than the Bible. They include such familiar sayings as:

- He who spares the rod hates his son, but he who loves him is careful to discipline him (13:24).
- A gentle answer turns away wrath, but a harsh word stirs up anger (15:1).
- A happy heart makes the face cheerful, but heartache crushes the spirit (15:13).
- Pride goes before destruction, a haughty spirit before a fall (16:18).
- A fool finds no pleasure in understanding but delights in airing his own opinions (18:2).

Proverbs such as the last ones were plentiful. They generally point out the disastrous end of those who don't pursue wisdom.

While the general tenor of the book of Proverbs is to collect such maxims that herald wisdom, the book of Job dramatizes the struggle between wisdom and chaos. If wisdom represents the perfect order, the ideal Christian state of being, then its adversary is the random disorder of chaos. Within that conflict afflicted Job, his three friends, and the young man Elihu come together. The story of Job's desolation anticipates Renaissance comedy, where the characters suffer hopeless disorder, only to have the herald (Elihu) come, and the divine figure (God/*deus ex machina*) arrive from above to establish order. In form and in argument, Job is a very puzzling but also a dazzling dramatic work. One could mine its wisdom for years without depleting the precious ore.

The monologue that shapes Ecclesiastes is also dramatic in nature, but it is interior, a drama in the narrator's mind. Confounded by the worldly scene he surveys, the narrator wonders whether there is any hope to pursue, any goal of worth. Perhaps everything is simply a maelstrom of circularity—what the narrator calls vanity. We can also call it futility and self-sufficiency, both much in evidence in our own age. In any event, the Teacher of Ecclesiastes is profoundly disillusioned with what he sees. His opening words are a lamentation: "Meaningless! Meaningless! Utterly meaningless! Everything is meaningless" (1:2).

The narrator of Ecclesiastes has a few rhetorical tricks up his sleeve. As his thoughts darken into pessimism, he begins to wonder if there is any light whatsoever in his survey of the world: "My mind still guiding me with wisdom, I wanted to see what was worthwhile for men to do under heaven during the few days of their lives" (2:3). He searches for certain common goals of humanity: to enjoy work, to pursue wealth, to practice wickedness, to be contentedly lazy. All are futile. Then, just as he has shattered all the human means to achieve happiness, and having established them as false expectations, the narrator takes a neck-breaking twist in the final chapter. *Before* others go on such a search, *before* they attempt to pursue one of these avenues for themselves, *before* doing anything, do this: "Remember your Creator in the days of your youth, before the days of trouble come" (12:1). The First Thing is God.

The narrator ends the book with that admonition. Yet he concludes chapter 12 with two parting comments worthy of note. In verse 11 he advises: "The words of the wise are like goads, their collected sayings like firmly embedded nails—given by one Shepherd. Be warned, my son, of anything in addition to them." Here at the end is what we should seek first. The first eleven chapters are like one long adverbial clause giving the cause or condition for the twelfth chapter.

Saint Paul on Wisdom

With a conservative view of the wisdom books, we rely on these three, again noting that there is considerable pressure to expand them to Psalms, Song of Solomon, and two Apocryphal books. Psalms and Song of Solomon, for example, are radically different in tone, genre, and message from the three books we have considered. Moreover, there are no overt pretensions to being a wisdom book in either one. Furthermore, Psalms consists of so many different uses of song, and so many different authors, that it is futile to squeeze it into the wisdom mold. Yet, and I don't think this is inconsistent, there is one expansion we have to make. The discussion in this biblical passage is dedicated to wisdom. It also opens new insights to understanding wisdom. I am thinking of Paul's wisdom discourse in 1 Corinthians, the first two chapters. Before we move on to consider further qualities of wisdom, it is worthwhile to briefly consider what Paul has to say.

Basically, Paul performs the great reversal. What seems foolish in the eyes of the world constitutes wisdom in the eyes of God. Paul begins in a typical manner, encouraging the Corinthians because "You do not lack any spiritual gift as you eagerly wait for our Lord Jesus Christ to be revealed" (1:7). Moreover, Paul adds that "He will keep you strong to the end, so that you will be blameless on the day of our Lord Jesus Christ" (1:8). With that reassurance for the present and for the future, Paul is ready to dive into his chosen topic. The topic is not a new one for Paul. He is often on the alert for pretenses from worldly sources that threaten the Christian community, and that pose challenges to his spiritual teaching.

In 1 Corinthians 1:.18 Paul makes what appears to be a stunning admission: "For the message of the cross is foolishness to those who are perishing, but to us who are being saved it is the power of God." From the point of view of secular wisdom, the idea (that Jesus died to save us from our sins) and the reality (the actual event of the cross) are a grand absurdity. The lyrical passage that follows in verses 26–31 develops the nature of the wise believer: "But God chose the foolish things of the world to shame the wise; God chose the weak things of the world to shame the strong. He chose the lowly things of this world and the despised things—and the things that are not—to nullify the things that are. . . . It is because of him that you are in Christ Jesus, who has become for us wisdom from God—that is, our righteousness, holiness, and redemption" (27–30). In Paul's mathematics, belief results in wisdom, while in the world's mathematics, wisdom equals belief. For Paul, commitment leads to understanding.

As he continues his argument into the second chapter of 1 Corinthians, Paul asserts that he came to them "in weakness and fear and with much trembling." Paul was a learned man, of course, and at times he even boasts of his great learning. We recall that Paul identified himself before the Sanhedrin as "I am a Pharisee, the son of a Pharisee" (Acts 23:6). Then he spoke from a position of power granted by his learning; now he testifies that he speaks "with a demonstration of the Spirit's power, so that your faith might not rest on men's wisdom, but on God's power" (1 Cor 2:4–5). Paul concludes his wisdom discourse by seeking the thoughts of God as revealed by the Spirit of God. Doing so results in the triumphant assertion that "We have the mind of Christ" (2:16).

Benjamin Franklin: The Perfectible Man

In 1784, while living near Paris, Benjamin Franklin turned once again to completing his on-again, off-again effort to write his *Autobiography*. By this point in his life, he was likely the best-known man in America, a veritable paragon of Enlightenment thinking, an acclaimed international statesman, and an inventor who would change the world. So what did he think of when he returned to his *Autobiography*? Just this: "It was about this time I conceived the bold and arduous project of arriving at moral perfection."[3] Enlightenment thinkers believed that with the right scientific strategy, personal dedication, and native intelligence, a state of moral perfection could be attained. Not surprisingly, Franklin continues with his strategy: "I wished to live without committing any fault any time; I would conquer all that either natural inclination, custom, or company might lead me into. As I knew, or thought I knew, what was right and wrong, I did not see why I might not always do the one and avoid the other" (307).

The point here is that Franklin really believed that he could achieve moral perfection, all on his own. No outside force was necessary. The Enlightenment person, of which there are a great many yet today, is wholly self-sufficient. Therefore, no savior is necessary, and God is merely a great deistic maker. He crafted the earth with its natural laws, then stepped aside to let the world run according to those laws. In deism there is no immanent God, no God with us, no Emmanuel, no Christmas and no Easter. Humanity, for better or worse, is on its own. It is telling that Franklin had to double down on his effort and compose a list of thirteen virtues to live by. There were twelve at first, but a friend pointed out that when he became perfect, he would probably be proud. So, Franklin added the thirteenth: "HUMILITY. Imitate Jesus and Socrates." There is no divinity in Franklin's Jesus. He is simply, like Socrates, a good moral teacher.

That Franklin was brilliant is hardly arguable. He is bedecked with achievements as if a great Christmas wreath spangled with flickering lights were draped across his shoulders. Indeed, after reading *Poor Richard's Almanack*, many might call him wise. Franklin's aphorisms have gone down into a common heritage of American wisdom. For example:

3. Franklin, *Autobiography*, 307. Future quotations from *Autobiography* will be cited parenthetically.

> "Eat to live, and not live to eat."
>
> "Early to bed and early to rise makes a man healthy, wealthy, and wise."
>
> "God helps them that help themselves."
>
> "Make haste slowly."[4]

It's simple folk wisdom, but by it Franklin acquired wealth and recognition.

The example of Ben Franklin is important to our purposes here. He certainly contributed to the modern American mind—the sense that I can do it all on my own. We moderns prize self-sufficiency. On the one hand, then, Franklin shows that God is lavish with his gifts, favoring who he will. Furthermore, God will use various means to carry out his purposes in the world, often in ways that are unexpected and surprising to us. Benjamin Franklin is a prooftext for common grace. But, on the other hand, he doesn't fit what the Bible calls "wisdom from above" (Jas 3:17). And our intention is to find out just what such "wisdom from above" is.

The Source of Wisdom

Our first step in pursuing that issue is to ask ourselves what the source of wisdom is. I hesitate to call it "spiritual wisdom," because, after all, wisdom is what it is no matter the context. Nonetheless, one of the most widely attested issues in all of Scripture is that the source of wisdom is in God. Regardless of how wisdom is used or intended on earth, its source is divine. Consider just a few sources from the Bible that testify to this fact.

In 1 Kings 3–4 we find recorded the story of the two women and the one living child. The women bring before Solomon the issue of who owns the baby. After his famous decision to prove the mother, a swell of admiration arises toward Solomon. The narrator, however, refines the admiration to its proper source: "When all Israel heard the verdict the king had given, they saw that he had wisdom from God to administer justice" (3:28). It is not surprising. We remember that Solomon had asked God for wisdom in governing the unruly Israelites.[5]

4. Franklin, *Poor Richard's Almanack*, 17–19.

5. Solomon, of course, was the hands-down winner in the wisdom sweepstakes. First Kings 4:29–30 reads: "God gave Solomon wisdom and very great insight and a breadth of understanding as measureless as the sand on the seashore. Solomon's wisdom was greater than the wisdom of all the men of the East, and greater than all the wisdom of Egypt."

Prior to his lessons in wisdom, James sets forth as a presupposition: "If any of you lacks wisdom, he should ask God, who gives generously to all without finding fault, and it will be given to him" (Jas 1:5). With that fact established James continues to discuss wisdom in the following chapters. We have already considered Paul's discourse on wisdom in 1 Corinthians, but two passages there are critical for the case that all wisdom is a gift from God. Paul speaks, for example, of the source of wisdom in 1 Corinthians 1:7–10: "We speak of God's secret wisdom, a wisdom that has been hidden and that God destined for our glory before time began. None of the rulers of this age understood it, for if they had, they would not have crucified the Lord of glory. . . . But God has revealed it to us by his Spirit." And again, in 1:13 Paul adds: "This is what we speak, not in words taught us by human wisdom but in words taught by the Spirit, expressing spiritual truths in spiritual words."

Calvin and the *Imago Dei*

As we seek the source of wisdom, then, we see its origins in God. This is the biblical pattern, beginning in Genesis 1:27: "God created man in his own image, in the image of God he created him; male and female he created them." Therefore, we speak of humankind bearing the *imago Dei*—the image of God, and we conclude that each human bears some likenesses to the God who created us. An imprint remains of the one Maker. Just as we can intuitively know that a painting is of Bosch, or Rembrandt, or Van Gogh, so we know that humanity is the creation of God.

Few theologians examined the *imago Dei* more carefully than John Calvin, for no matter how pessimistic he was about fallen humanity, he was optimistic that God indwelt humanity through the image of God.[6] Calvin's discussion appears in two primary places in *The Institutes*. In the first of these, appearing in I.iii, Calvin argues that humanity has a

6. Gerard Manley Hopkins wrote in "God's Grandeur":

> There lives the dearest freshness deep down things;
> And though the last lights off the black West went
> Oh, morning, at the brown brink eastwards, springs—
> Because the Holy Ghost over the bent
> World broods with warm breast and ah! bright wings.

That "brooding spirit," in the estimation of Calvin as well as Hopkins, remains active within us (Hopkins, "God's Grandeur," 128).

natural instinct for God. This is the starting point for his proofs for God's existence: "We lay it down as a position not to be controverted, that the human mind, even by natural instinct, possesses some sense of a Deity. For that no man might shelter himself under the pretext of ignorance, God hath given to all some apprehension of his existence."[7] The natural question that follows is where does this "natural instinct" come from? Obviously, it does not arise from one's natural state, else we could as likely be discoursing with elephants and baboons about the nature of God. It would have to arise outside humanity but be imbued within humanity. Thus, God is the author of the image of God within us.

Thereby Calvin develops the source of the *imago Dei.* Remaining is the issue of what exactly constitutes that image. Calvin begins with the presupposition: "That man consists of soul and body, ought not to be controverted. By the 'soul' I understand an immortal, yet created essence, which is the nobler part of him. . . . Though the glory of God is displayed in the external form, yet there is no doubt that the proper seat of his image is in the soul" (I.xv.2). This, in Calvin's estimation, is what distinguishes us from the animal kingdom. So we have the "where," but we also need the "what." Basically, Calvin holds that the image of God consists of an order or harmony in humanity that embodies God's perfect design: "The image of God . . . denotes the integrity which Adam possessed, when he was endued with a right understanding, when he had affections regulated by reason, and all his senses governed in proper order" (I.xv.3). As we know, and according to Calvin, when Adam fell to temptation, he began a process of "alienation" from the image of God. But with Jesus's incarnation, crucifixion, and resurrection a process of "regeneration" was begun, so that "Christ may form us anew in the image of God" (I.xv.4).

The Qualities of Wisdom

If we find, then, that the source of true wisdom lies in God, we are faced with the question of what purpose is wisdom. It's a nice gift, an answer to prayer, but what do we do with it? Consider the fact that in secular eyes the nature of wisdom differs a bit. In fact, it seems that synonyms apply, not true wisdom. In the world we find terms like *craftiness, shrewdness,*

7. Calvin, *Compend of The Institutes,* I.iii.1. Further quotations will be cited parenthetically. I am using this well-known *Compend* in this essay for the sake of brevity and accuracy. Calvin waxes prolix whenever he discusses wisdom. Kerr nicely reveals the essence of his thought in somewhat more lucid prose.

canniness, or *cleverness*. But those terms are not at all the same as wisdom. They originate in the world and are practicalities learned from experience. Spiritual wisdom may be distinguished by its own qualities and purposes. Of these many qualities, four stand in the foreground: righteousness, understanding, actions, and skill or talent.

As we live in wisdom, we stand in righteousness. Wisdom gives us the ability to discern right from wrong, and the reasoning ability to choose the right. Clearly this is what Paul had in mind when he wrote in Philippians 1:9–11: "And this is my prayer: that your love may abound more and more in knowledge and depth of insight, so that you may be able to discern what is best and may be pure and blameless until the day of Christ, filled with the fruit of righteousness that comes through Jesus Christ—to the glory and praise of God." This knowledge is not unique to Paul. Two passages in the Old Testament express the same thought. Proverbs 2:9–11 puts it like this: "Then you will understand what is right and just and fair—every good path. For wisdom will enter your heart, and knowledge will be pleasant to your soul. Discretion will protect you, and understanding will guard you." Shortly after, we find: "Trust in the Lord with all your heart and lean not on your own understanding; in all your ways acknowledge him, and he will make your paths straight" (Prov 3:5–6).

Righteousness is marked by the ability to discern right from wrong and to make the right choice. It is following God's will in the busy avenues of this world. We need God's wisdom "to make our paths straight." But we also need God's gift of wisdom to live knowledgeably. Knowledge is something we acquire. It is a body of events, experiences, and facts. But to employ that knowledge judiciously we need "the wisdom from above." Knowledge for knowledge's sake, or for the sake of profit, is the hallmark of worldly wisdom. We celebrate those individuals who know a lot. They appear on game shows and win a lot of money. Worldly wisdom is all about getting ahead.

Divine wisdom, however, tells us how to live properly with the knowledge we acquire. Again, Philippians gives a nice definition of wisdom and knowledge: "And this is my prayer: that your love may abound more and more in knowledge and depth of insight, so that you may be able to discern what is best and may be pure and blameless until the day of Christ, filled with the fruit of righteousness that comes through Jesus Christ—to the glory and praise of God" (1:9–11).

An interesting avenue of thought arises from that passage. It has to do with knowledge and action. If, as Paul says, we pursue wisdom to honor Jesus, then there also appears to be a contrary wisdom that comes from below and that aims to honor oneself. James touches upon this in his analysis of wisdom. In 3:13–15 James writes: "Who is wise and understanding among you? Let him show it by his good life, by deeds done in the humility that comes from wisdom. But if you harbor bitter envy and selfish ambition in your hearts, do not boast about it or deny the truth. Such wisdom does not come down from heaven but is earthly, unspiritual, of the devil." James is not alone. The whole of Proverbs 9 is an extended comparison between the soundness of wisdom's knowledge and the folly and lack of judgment in worldly wisdom. Therefore, we can say that nearly without exception one will know them by their fruits (Matt 7:16). Our actions are the public face of the wisdom we harbor within.

Knowledge may well be seen as independent from wisdom, and some argue that the word *understanding* should be used. The distinction drives at the fact that wisdom is not mere intelligence—a body of knowledge that has been mastered. Examples abound all around us. For one example, consider the Unabomber Ted Kaczynski, who enrolled in Harvard at age sixteen. Widely considered a math prodigy, with an IQ score somewhere in the 150s, Ted used his prodigious knowledge to blow things up. One could doubt his wisdom. Understanding, we might say, is knowing the proper use and purpose of knowledge. We also observe that many of the biblical passages encouraging us to seek wisdom link it with understanding (see Job 28:12; Prov 3:12; Isa 11:2; Eph 1:8). The point is that wisdom is not static; it is acted out in this world through the knowledge and understanding we might have.

Through the years of our marriage, my wife and I have taken a once or twice weekly "date night." This is nothing elaborate; it's just a matter of taking time to spend it together. Sometimes we'll ride out to the Lake Michigan shore or take a backroad nature ride. We always wind up at a good restaurant to enjoy a meal. She's the driver, so often gets the choice of where to go. I mention the fact not for any wisdom intrinsic to it, but because of the way ideas can come to light. We were talking about wisdom and evidences of it one day, when Pat observed that the fruit of the Spirit in Galatians 5 is the clearest evidence of wisdom. If we believe James that wisdom is "full of mercy and good fruit," then I think she was on the right track.

The listing of the fruit of the Spirit is preceded by two essential stipulations. The first is that Jesus has liberated us by his life and death: "It is for freedom that Christ has set us free. Stand firm, then, and do not let yourselves be burdened again by a yoke of slavery" (Gal 5:1). The fruit, then, are part of a liberated life, a life freely chosen rather than imposed upon us like some country club dues. The second stipulation appears in verse 6: "The only thing that counts is faith expressing itself through love." As we move into the life by the Spirit section of Galatians 5, we already know that it is freely chosen and that it is chosen out of love, important qualifications for understanding the beauty of the fruit. After listing qualities of a disbelieving and immoral age, Paul turns to the fruit. I list them for reference as they appear in Galatians 5:22–23: "The fruit of the Spirit is love, joy, peace, patience, kindness, goodness, faithfulness, gentleness and self-control. Against such things there is no law." Differing passages of the Bible may slightly add to or qualify this fundamental list.

As we examined the purposes or qualities of wisdom, we observe three in particular: 1) seeking righteousness, whereby the individual spirit is aligned with God; 2) accumulating knowledge or understanding to live in discernment; and 3) committing right actions, guided by the fruit of the spirit. In all these we see that wisdom is a gift from God. That raises the subject of a special sort of wisdom, which is also a gift from God. Although we don't think of this gift very often, it is essential for living in God's grace and, as the *Heidelberg Catechism* has it, enjoying him forever. This special wisdom or grace is the skill or talent for artmaking.

As the Israelite nation settled down after its wars and long journeys, it was time to solidify its spiritual government. At that time Israel was a theocracy, a nation governed by God through anointed persons. Moreover, the tabernacle was to be constructed in such a way that the glory of the Lord was manifested through it. To that end, God invested craftsmen with special skills, knowledge, and talents to make art. The first step was to be the priestly garments: "Tell all the skilled men to whom I have given wisdom in such matters that they are to make garments for Aaron for his consecration, so he may serve me as priest" (Exod 28:3). The rest of the chapter consists of intricate directions for making the priestly garments.

The same artmaking wisdom is visited upon other craftsmen, particularly Bezalel and Oholiab, as they prepare to build the tabernacle. Moses announces them like this: "See, the Lord has chosen Bezalel son of Uri, the son of Hur, of the tribe of Judah, and he has filled him with the Spirit of

God, with skill, ability and knowledge in all kinds of crafts—to make artistic designs for work in gold, silver and bronze" (Exod 35:30–32). Oholiab is included in the artmaking in the next verse.

The Emmanuel

We see, then, that wisdom has certain identifiable qualities. Furthermore, having been created in the image of God, we are able to comprehend those qualities and to live by them. But we would be remiss if we failed to account for the presence of Wisdom in our daily lives. I am referring here to one who is greater than the whole of the qualities we have discussed. I am referring, in fact, to the Son of God, who lived among us to do the Father's will, and whose teachings and actions live today through the words of his Holy Book.

Although any of the Gospels provides unique insights into Jesus's character, and although any New Testament epistle sheds light on Jesus's beliefs and life, I want to focus for a moment on the Gospel of John, and that at the very start: "In the beginning was the Word, and the Word was with God, and the Word was God. He was with God in the beginning" (John 1:1–2). Peter said: "We did not follow cleverly invented stories when we told you about the power and coming of our Lord Jesus Christ, but we were eyewitnesses of his majesty" (2 Peter 1:16). The verse from John is testimony to that majesty. It claims that the Word—the Greek *Logos* or "rational underpinning" of the world, here used for Jesus—is eternal. Moreover, this Jesus is God, albeit in a separate person from the Father. He is one with and yet other than God the Father and God the Holy Spirit. And he was there with God when the world was created: "Through him all things were made; without him nothing was made that has been made. In him was life, and that life was the light of men" (John 1:3).

John's elucidation of the divinity of Jesus is abetted later in the Gospel when John the Baptist arrives on the scene. He states that "The one whom God has sent speaks the words of God, for God gives the Spirit without limit. The Father loves the Son and has placed everything in his hands. Whoever believes in the Son has eternal life, but whoever rejects the Son will not see life, for God's wrath remains on him" (John 3:35–36). Jesus, then, comes with divine wisdom, and the purpose of that wisdom is to grant eternal life. Jesus himself was not at all shy about testifying to his divinity and spiritual wisdom. For example, we read in John 14:6: "I am the way and the truth and the life. No one comes to the Father except through me."

When we seek wisdom, then, we do well to seek first the words of Jesus. He speaks to us in parables and stories, in figurative language and plain address. Always his words are freighted with wisdom. And why not? It is apparent that on every day of his earthly life Jesus was mindful of his heavenly mission. He walked the hot country of his birth telling others that in him was eternal life. But that wasn't all of it. He lived out eternal wisdom in daily events. He championed the poor, the neglected, and the lonely. He healed those who had escaped official notice and who lived out of the public spotlight. He himself "Being in very nature God, did not consider equality with God something to be grasped, but made himself nothing, taking the very nature of a servant" (Phil 2:6-7). That is the way of wisdom, but the way doesn't end there, for

> God exalted him to the highest place
> And gave him the name that is above every name,
> That at the name of Jesus every knee should bow,
> In heaven and on earth and under the earth,
> and every tongue confess that Jesus Christ is Lord,
> to the glory of God the Father.
> (Phil 2:9-11)

The wonder of divine wisdom is that Jesus, the source of our wisdom, is alive today, where, as he says, he intercedes for us before God the Father.

Chapter Ten

The Promise of Peace

It doesn't take a poetic mind to see the expressway on a crowded afternoon as a metaphor for life. The hurry, the noise, the unexpected maneuvers of automobiles sliding among lanes, all in a fierce hurry to get somewhere first.

As I weave through the expressway's twists and turns, bellowing semitrucks riding on each side, my mind is on something else. How very much it seems like each small automobile or wallowing truck is a world unto itself, swirling through the stars, on no certain path. There is absolutely no connectedness, no neighborliness possible on the freeway. My Ford better not shake hands with your GMC. Each driver speeds along, encased in steel and glass, utterly alone.

I turn now onto a quiet residential street along Riverside Park. Over my left shoulder I catch glimpses of the shining, swollen river, broad shouldered with spring runoff. All the trees hold bunches of new leaves as they line the riverbank.

The tan, brick building rises like an exclamation mark on the right. Four stories of windows shine with the late afternoon sun. The entrance, nearly buried by oak and maple, opens onto a pot-holed road. From the moment I turn onto it time seems otherworldly, oddly suspended like the lives within this West Michigan Home for Veterans. To alleviate the unbroken sameness of the building, someone erected a soaring aluminum sculpture in front of the entrance. I heard that it was supposed to be the prow of a ship soaring over the crashing waves. It looked like a left-over construction project.

The grounds are eerily quiet. I park under a small sign: "No Veteran Dies Alone." My car points at a groundskeeper kneeling in a large oval garden. He is planting pink and white begonias in concentric rows. Mechanically, he trowels out a deep clod of black earth, sets the plant, shakes the dirt back in. Several more gardens wait to be planted. In the distance stands a John Deere yard machine hitched to a trailer overflowing with flower trays. The groundskeeper will be at it for awhile.

I sit in the car for a moment, allowing the strange sense of unease to dissipate. It is an anxiety that has grown with each mile. Even after months of doing this volunteer work, I still feel some anxiety when I pull onto the entrance road. I picture Room 412, my destination. I picture the dying man I will tend to for the next two hours, what he will look like, what stage of dying he is going through. I wonder if everybody in our small group of about twenty members feels this way. As always, the preliminaries nearly do me in.

I take the stairs to the fourth floor today. My "No Veteran Dies Alone" lanyard and logoed blue shirt provide unquestioned admittance to any floor. The smells seem to intensify the higher up one goes. I sneeze as I open the fourth floor doorway. I greet the people at the nurses' station. Room 412 is just a few doors down.

He will be alone, unless the previous watchkeeper is still with him. We come to those who have outlived friends, whose family is distant or absent, those who would otherwise die alone in a barren room. The room is neat and clean, smelling unobtrusively of disinfectants.

My veteran is curled under a light blanket. He is devoid of tubes and machines now. All he is being given are morphine and lorazepam. His eyes are closed. He is in a coma now. His eyes will not open again in this life. He is what we refer to as "actively dying."

I sit down, reach across his body, and hold his hand. It is limp. And cold. His skin is the dusky gray of old granite, weathered and wrinkled. I can't help wondering: Did he once hold the hand of a parent, feeling secure? Did his hand tingle when he held the hand of a young woman for the first time? There is no return pressure from him now.

I talk to him—about the weather, about the traffic, about the trees, about whatever crosses my mind. He can't speak, but it is uncertain how much he can hear. There is a general belief that hearing is the last sense a dying person loses, even while in a final coma. So I keep talking, letting him know he is not alone.

It is remarkable how your own concerns diminish when tending the dying.

Above his bed a small plaque is held to the wall with glue strips. It looks like a homemade craft, probably by some well-intended member of a church guild or association. Hand-painted flags wave forever at the sides. At the center arises his name in relief: "Martin."

I try to imagine what this unseeing, maybe unhearing, waiting Martin was like as a child. I picture him running on a playground, blue jeans and holey tennis shoes, trying to get a kite to fly. Was he shy, or outgoing? Did he play catch with a tennis ball against the garage door, or did he have buddies to play with? I picture him driving his first car. Then driving it to the Enlistment Office.

Alongside the bed stands a small end table. On it are a portable CD player, a stack of CDs of the country and southern gospel variety, and a bag with items to pass the time. Crossword puzzle books, a tablet of lined paper, pencils, some odds and ends. And, oh yes. What we refer to as "the journal." It contains notes taken when each attendant came on duty, the calendar of people on this watch, notes on his condition. Any changes. That sort of thing.

I mostly wait in the chair, leaning forward to hold the veteran's hand, talking now and then as the Spirit moves me, watching the slow, tell-tale rise and fall of the blanket. At different times I move into prayer for Martin.

Always, at the close of my shift, I stand, place my hand on the dying one's forehead, and murmur into the silence these words:

> The Lord bless you and keep you;
> The Lord make his face shine upon you
> And be gracious to you;
> The Lord turn his face toward you
> And give to you his peace.

Words of grace to live by and to die by. They are the words of grace as we move through our daily tasks, as we lay ourselves down to sleep, during the still hours when no sleep comes. God keeps us; his face shines upon us; he is gracious to us.

When I move back under the aluminum sculpture toward my car, it has grown dark. And raining. Just a soft, insistent spring rain. I bet the begonias are dancing in their beds. I am too tired to hurry, and the rain rivulets down my neck and under my collar.

I have just come down from the dying. Grant us your peace.

* * * * *

Peace is God's gift. Elusive, intangible, yet peace is something everyone longs for. We long for it for our own sake; we try, occasionally, to bestow it upon others. And sometimes we echo Job: "What I feared has come upon me; what I dreaded has happened to me. I have no peace, no quietness; I have no rest, but only turmoil" (Job 3:25–26).

You can't measure out peace like a bag of coins. In fact, most people would agree that peace can't be bought. That is an oddity in an age where nearly everything else can be.

Ralph Waldo Emerson, whose life spanned most of the nineteenth century (1803–1882), observed in "Self-Reliance" that "Nothing can bring you peace but yourself."[1] Even given the fact that Emerson stood far to the left of liberal politics, and also that he was capable of such crackpot statements as "I become a transparent eye-ball. I am nothing. I see all," Emerson's view of peace is pretty much the standard of today.[2] The problem is that this view confuses peace with happiness. If you can afford to do all those things that give you pleasure, then categorically you are probably happy. However, that does not equate to peace. Peace is a state of soul.

So our first thought is that a state of peace is not necessarily defined by being happy. Now, surely one can be happy and in a state of peace also. That's a fine place to be. Some are blessed by it, and the rest of us enjoy the vice of envy. Even more dangerous, however, are those who equate biblical peace with political peace. Surely political peace, or at least peace among nations, is a good thing, we might protest. Indeed, it is. War is a horror incarnate. Only in recent years have we fully appreciated that the toll on those who are sent to war does not end when they come home or when the war ends. The effects are lifelong and devastating.

Many of the references to peace in the Bible are of a political sort. The book, after all, records a history, and a meaningful portion of that history

1. Emerson, "Self-Reliance," 1350.

2. Emerson, "Nature," 1284. Emerson continues his list of claims as this line continues: "The currents of the Universal Being circulate through me; I am part or particle of God."

involved wars, especially to establish the promised land. Thus, we find in Genesis 26:28–29 Abimelech's words to Isaac: "Let us make a treaty with you that you will do us no harm, just as we did not molest you but always treated you well and sent you away in peace. And now you are blessed by the Lord." The Old Testament writers were intent on their task to record peace treaties among warring nations, boundary markers to prevent disputes, and immanent threats to an established peace.

Such also is the peace we long for and treasure when we have it. If our past century proved anything to us it was that we stood on a very slippery slope. Wars raged around and below us and often they swept us into their maw.[3] We prized those moments when peace held fast, however briefly. Thus far in an equally difficult twenty-first century, our nation has taken on the role of enablers of war. We supply the war materiel to selected nations in their wars. We are hardly champions of peace. All of the political peace that we long for is still a far cry from what Isaiah had in mind when he said,

> You will keep in perfect peace
> Him whose mind is steadfast
> Because he trusts in you.
> (Isa 6:3)

Isaiah speaks of the peace of a steadfast mind, at peace in calm or war because it doesn't depend upon changing events around us but on the unchanging Lord.

3. In the case of the United States, a couple of items are necessary to keep the record of political peace accurate. Our many national actions of war constitute an historical irony. The Delegates to the Constitutional Convention in 1787 very deliberately reserved the right to declare war for Congress (Article 1, Section 8, Clause 11). It was a bold move to limit the power of the president, and to keep it in the hands of the people. It didn't work, of course, since as commanders-in-chief of the armed forces, presidents have sent us into war countless times, using such terms as "incursion," "conflict," and "military aid" instead of "war." Surprisingly, Congress has only declared war eleven times in our history, almost always unanimously except for the contentious War of 1812.

Furthermore, our first president adamantly held that the country should not get involved in alliances with foreign nations—in addition to those already established.

The thought was that we should at all costs avoid involvement in the wars of other nations. In George Washington's remarkable *Farewell Address* (recorded in Senate on September 19, 1796), he declared: "Observe good faith and justice towards all nations; cultivate peace and harmony with all—religion and morality enjoin this conduct; and can it be that good policy does not equally enjoin it?" The remarkable quality of his address is the large respect for religion in the first half of the document and the ardor for isolationism in the second.

Saint Augustine was one of the first to develop what we might call a "Christian theology of war." He pondered whether war was permissible, whether peace was achievable. In Book 19 of *City of God*, Augustine provided his fullest treatment of peace, the very goal and central characteristic of the city of God. For Augustine, what we know about peace in our earthly kingdom of God, is also what we know about eternity. Therefore, "Peace between a mortal man and his Maker consists in ordered obedience, guided by faith, under God's eternal law. . . . The peace of the heavenly city lies in a perfectly ordered and harmonious communion of those who find their joy in God and in one another in God. Peace, in its final sense, is the calm that comes of order."[4] It was Augustine's habit to develop his argument by what I call "accumulation." Contrary to the building steps of traditional and logical argument, Augustine feeds additional information into a previous argument at disparate points in his text. Sometimes it tends to make his arguments a bit unwieldy. But of his views on war and peace, Augustine would always say that God is the creator of order. When he created all things, he called them good, which meant that each individual part was fitting or harmonious with the whole. While fallen humanity tends toward disorder, and therefore we experience war, we still pursue that first created order of God. Thus, the city of God modeled on God's order. Thus, too, peace. Although it might be better to use the Old Testament word *shalom* to characterize the city of God.

In *Journey Toward Justice*, Nicholas Wolterstorff points out that "Shalom goes beyond peace, beyond the absence of hostility. A nation may be at peace and yet be miserable in its poverty. Shalom is not just peace but flourishing, flourishing in all dimensions of our existence—in our relation to God, in our relation to our fellow human beings, in our relation to ourselves, in our relation to creation in general."[5] The benefit of using this Old Testament concept that Wolterstorff describes is that it helps us understand that peace is much more than merely the absence of war. Surely that absence is something we long for, especially in an age when war is sudden. It tends to sneak up on us around the corner and

4. Augustine, *City of God*, 456. Augustine is best remembered for his claim that all war is for peace: "What then, men want in war is that it should end in peace. Even while waging a war every man wants peace, whereas no one wants war while he is making peace" (452). In our age, and possibly in Augustine's too, war is always about power first, and land secondly. Seldom do wars end in peace.

5. Wolterstorff, *Journey Toward Justice*, 114.

take us by surprise. Then it is there, staring us in the eyes with steely resolve. We long for peace; we hope for *shalom*.

Our first point, then, is that peace is not necessarily a state of being happy. Nor, secondly, is it to be understood as political peace, or an absence of war. As admirable as these two states are, neither is a formula for spiritual peace. To define: "Inner peace is a state of calm and assurance given by God and nurtured by his Word." This peace is not a rational process. One does not achieve it by logic or by argument. This much is clear in Philippians 4: 6–7: "Do not be anxious about anything, but in everything, by prayer and petition, with thanksgiving, present your requests to God. And the peace of God, which transcends all understanding, will guard your hearts and your minds in Christ Jesus." This passage is also used as the blessing on Holy Communion in *The Book of Common Prayer*, and is frequently used as a benediction. But what a marvelous passage—majestic in its scope but as tender and personal as your own soul. Peace is a guard on your soul, put in place by Jesus himself.

One of Jesus's best-known benedictions appears in his farewell address to his disciples, which includes us: "Peace I leave with you; my peace I give you. I do not give to you as the world gives. Do not let your hearts be troubled and do not be afraid" (John 14:27). From the start, then, divine peace, the kind we are working to define here, is different from the world's understanding of peace. This much we have established so far. Furthermore, we argued that divine peace, the sort given by Jesus, is a state of mind. It is not determined by world events such as wealth, happiness, or freedom from conflict. All these are nice indeed, but they are not the subject of our discussion here. What we are concerned about is the God-given peace that results in a certain state of mind. That state of mind is powerful, of course. We are not talking about a benign daydream or happy reminiscence. We are talking about a mind that shapes all of our actions, allegiances, and the very beliefs we live by and that give our living meaning. Now we examine exactly what constitutes that state of mind, or what its qualities or characteristics are like. Without coming to some agreement about that, we may as well be talking about water for breakfast and a slice of bread for supper—very little by way of substance.

The very first quality of this peace is a life of prayer. Few things are more active and tiring than prayer. I may receive a gift of a new basketball (the Wilson NBA official game basketball at $199.95, since we are hypothesizing) but that basketball will do me very little good unless I get out in the driveway and practice dribbling and shooting. My whole body has to get in tune with its muscle memory. Think of prayer as a muscle. The more you exercise it and practice it, the stronger it grows.

Prayer begins, when one is out of practice, in fits and starts. One will find the mind slipping and sliding like a Michigan winter. It will also be nearly as void of growth. This is natural and nothing really to be afraid of. But it must be mastered. The easiest (and probably most effective) way to do that is to keep a written prayer list. A second, and slightly more detailed, practice is to write out your prayers during a time of devotions. I use a small, spiral-bound notebook for each recording. Both of these protocols effectively harness the brain's tendency to wander about rather aimlessly. Both help us remember and focus.

Keeping a prayer list and writing out our prayers are both effective for a hearty prayer life. However, it is necessary to add a third qualification; that is, the mindfulness that we are speaking with God. I find sometimes that my mind is going in circles and that my prayers never escape my own skull. Or, I may feel that I am praying to myself or to others, and not to God. That is why I often have to work on the mindfulness that I am praying to God. Fully grasping that miracle is a wonderful task—I am praying to the King of creation, to Jesus the Lord of heaven and earth, through the power and mercy of the Holy Spirit.

This is what is meant, I believe, by Psalm 46:10–11: "Be still, and know that I am God; I will be exalted among the nations, I will be exalted in the earth. The Lord Almighty is with us; the God of Jacob is our fortress." This is an awesome privilege and shouldn't be undertaken lightly. When I pray, I am in the presence of God. Such an enormous, such an audacious, task is not to be met casually. It requires, at the least, some preparation of soul and mind, some order of praise and petition, and some keen attention. But it is precisely at such a state that God breathes peace into a believer's mind.

Our first step toward this inner state of peace, then, is the exercise of meaningful prayer. This nurtures our divine relationship with God. In the routine cycles of our lives, God can seem distant, our contact with him more tense and fractured. In time there is no contact at all. This seems to be the case in other contemporary attitudes. A popular refrain among some believers these days runs like this: "I'm a Christian, but I don't go to church." I assume, perhaps wrongfully, that the speaker also has diminished contact with the Redeemer, the very basis of belief and church. Churchgoing is simply one more way of exercising one's spiritual muscle. In Acts 10:

36 Luke writes: "You know the message God sent to the people of Israel, telling the good news of peace through Jesus Christ, who is Lord of all." But if you're not in prayer, and if you're not in church, it's likely that you don't know the good news of peace very well.

Finally, the avenues ordered toward a state of peace, or being in peace, that have been raised thus far ideally ought to make some impact on ordering our personal lives. As we saw earlier, Saint Augustine believed that the city of God on earth should mirror qualities of God's heavenly city. The view seems fully applicable today. The point is worth mentioning for the present age, as we have often seen in previous chapters, insists upon immediate gratification of personal needs and desires. A long, dark streak of selfishness mars contemporary civilization at all levels, from the halls of power to the hallways of despair. But we have the reminder of 1 Corinthians 14:33 that "God is not a God of disorder but of peace." Disorder seems like the rule today.

Order in American society stems from abiding by a central principle or set of principles. Therefore, the ordering principle of United States society is the Constitution and whatever laws Congress makes that meet the test of constitutionality. That is *practical* law; it tells us what is proper or improper for daily living in community. The aim is to promote decorum (or proper behavior), commonality (we are all subject to one set of laws), and protection (to prevent one person from abusing the rights of another). If that set of laws is well-crafted, and leaves room for exigencies, then we will have a lawful or orderly society. But not all people always follow even the best intended and most carefully constructed body of laws. Therefore, the law itself, like the Constitution, carries within it the provision of police and military bodies to enforce the law when individuals set themselves over community. In such a way we have practical order in society. In such a way, we intend to propagate a state of peace, understood here as freedom from harm or abuse of individual rights.

The peace that ensues from a life ordered according to some central, unifying document such as a constitution is a peace predicated upon understanding. It is only effective when the laws are understood and followed by the public. But what about the peace of God, that "which passes all understanding"? That too derives from the central order of law, in this case, the divine order of God's law as stated in Scripture and revealed by the Holy Spirit. This order consists not just in the central Ten Commandments, the centerpiece of God's law, but indeed throughout the Scripture which serves the Christian community as a sacred constitution. It also emanates from that moral gift in us called a conscience, particularly as it is informed by the Holy Spirit. If prayer is essential for us to be included in the community of God, what we might call "God's Holy People," then study of the Bible tells us how to live as a Holy People. This is the way to be "in peace."

Dante's *The Divine Comedy* is one of the great gifts to the literary and religious worlds. At one point in my early career, I felt a compelling urge to learn the trilogy as a whole. I had read parts and passages of each book but had never engaged a systematic study of the whole. So it was eventually that a group of about eight or ten of us like-minded teachers met to study a canto a week. In such a way we spent three delightful years studying Dante over lunch. In a work as long and complex as the *Comedy,* so called because it goes through terror to arrive at blessed peace, many themes emerge. As the reader finally enters *Paradise*, however, these lines guide the path:

> And please the King that here in-willeth us
> To His own will; and His will is our peace;
> This is the sea whereunto all things fare
> That it creates or nature furnishes.[6]

"His will is our peace": that finally is the goal of the Christian's quest for peace.

It also marks the last characteristic of divine peace that I wish to discuss here, and that is contentment. The logical progression here is straightforward, for if we are in God's will, we will necessarily achieve contentment. Frankly, it is a struggle sometimes to live in God's will. You can't just flip a switch some night and say, "Now I'm going to go and live in God's will for a while." It takes all the steps we have covered here. It's a matter of deliberation, of prayer, of coaching and study. Perhaps hardest of all, it is also a matter of surrendering our will for in "His will is our peace." As Paul wrote to Timothy, "Godliness with contentment is great gain. For we brought nothing into the world, and we can take nothing out of it" (1 Tim 6:6). But I don't think the alternative is very attractive either.

6. Dante, *Divine Comedy 3: Paradise*, Canto Three, II.84–87. Sayers's annotations always prove fascinating and are part of the enduring value of this text. Of this critical verse, Sayers writes: "In this famous utterance Piccarda sums up the very essence and nature of Paradise. In the identity of the souls' will with the will of God reside the perfection of their joy and the utter fulfillment of their desire" (79).

Shakespeare introduced the phrase "Now is the winter of our discontent."[7] John Steinbeck liked the line so much that he titled his last novel *The Winter of Our Discontent*. For Steinbeck especially, that winter is a symbol for the cold and arid moral landscape of modern American civilization. People live by cheating, lying, and chasing the dollar rather than contentment. There is no satisfaction; no warmth of human kindness; no rest; and especially no divine grace.

That is the secular alternative to the peace of God which passes all understanding. The steps that I have examined here seem to me to be rudimentary but essential for finding contentment in God's peace. Such a life is not a matter of whimsy, as if to say, "I'll try God's way now." Rather, it is a studied commitment. It also comes with a responsibility to live in peace with and to bring peace to others. We are called to practice the peace we find in Jesus. We are bringers of shalom. Matthew 5:9 has it like this: "Blessed are the peacemakers, for they shall be called children of God." If we understand divine peace rightly, we are blessed with peace and are expected to exercise peace by being peacemakers in the lives of others. Finally, then, the joy of peace is both that we live in God's peace, but also that we are empowered to bring that peace into the world. Taken together, we can discover that rarest form of peace: peace of mind. It brings to mind my back porch, from which I can observe the ceaseless activities of the backyard.

* * * * *

Wistful. A good word for the last day of the year.

December 31, 2024. I stand in the cold of the three-season porch, watching snow flurries tumble around the backyard like new puppies. After two days of rain, before the cold spell hit, the lawn was a sea of mud. Deer tracks sink down two inches. They visit every morning and evening, checking out dessert in my perennial garden. It's pretty slim pickings in winter, but they come anyway. Right now, three turkeys are noshing in the dirt under the bird feeders. Those horny feet can scoop out a load of dirt and fling it aside in reckless abandon. They are mammoth creatures, and ugly, the stuff of a cartoonist's dream.

7. Shakespeare, *King Richard the Third*, Act I, Scene I.I.1. There is some irony in the use of this sentence, for the next line states that the "Sun of York," or Richard, will melt the winter of our discontent.

God must have found some form and comeliness in them. I can't. Not even in that jaunty young male with his tail all aflutter, wooing the feathers off a hen that outweighs him by fifteen pounds.

Actually, at the moment I'm standing before the wall of glass wondering whether backyard is one word or two words. And then I am forced to sit down. I fall a lot. And I'm not particular about place or circumstances. I have fallen in my garden. I have fallen in the living room when it was full of company. I have broken eight ribs in falls now, two of them at once when I tried to step into beach sand to feel what it was like. I couldn't feel anything except my ribs cracking as I pitched over.

Even as I stand here, pain crawls along the spine with its fractured and collapsing vertebrae, along its surgical scars, out to my hips, up to my neck and a million nerve endings. According to the Veterans Administration I am 80 percent disabled. I wonder how they got it so low. After all, they're the ones who started it all anyway by drafting me and then flying me to a country where things went boom in the night.

And today—today is New Year's Eve and I am about to go to my bed and thank God for the sheer, undiluted happiness I feel. I will not kneel, for I can't get up. It becomes the disabled person's cry of survival: Never go somewhere you can't get up or out from. You never sit in chairs without arms. Never, ever, sit on a sofa. Never kneel.

It is good to sit, to watch flights of birds attack the feeders. A big northern flicker lands precariously on the finch feeder, his two-inch beak expertly snaring the tiny thistle feed. Two female goldfinches, now in their dusty gray winter coats, feed on the other side of the big bird.

For nearly forty years we have lived in this house. On every weekday until the little heater can't drive the cold away, my wife and I have eaten lunch out here on the porch. We watch the bird traffic in the backyard. In the late summer several of my thirty-five roses stand over seven feet high. They stretch above the wire deer fence, and I let them. The deer will do some fine dining.

On a day like this, a line from an e.e. cummings poem echoes: "I thank You God for most this amazing day."[8]

A hawk perches on the fence and all the feeders fall quiet. The bird looks like a sculpture, cold and heartless. It probably knows where the fluffle of rabbits hides out and is biding its time. I have had to bury several half-eaten rabbit corpses left in the backyard. Contrary to the belief that

8. cummings, "I Thank You God," 75.

hawks are dainty eaters, the ones around here are slobs. There is just too much food. Squirrels, rabbits, and small birds abound. Even a chipmunk or two for a late snack.

But I was well on my way to sleep by then. I can sleep at nearly any still moment, anytime, except at night. Strange impulses drive my limbs to flail about, much against my will. My leaden nerves are ornery, awakening at unguarded moments to torment me. I get up. I prowl around the house, fix a snack, read, until exhaustion creeps in and I head back to bed.

So now I look through the back window and it is New Year's Day, a morning full of snow and mischief. A flaming red cardinal huddles in the birch tree. He will sit there all morning, occasionally floating down to the snow under the feeder to filch a sunflower seed. One of my favorites, a tufted titmouse, is at the feeder. So beautiful, it is the pinup bird of the backyard.

The cardinal has barely finished his chorus when his dusky mate flies to the branch below him. They can't mate in the cold, but they sure keep romance alive. The ruddy male swoops to the snow beneath the feeder, snatches a sunflower seed, flies back to his mate, and feeds it to her. For all the world it looks like a kiss.

A vast quiet passes over the backyard. Creeping feet quiet. Birds wait patiently. The verse in Psalm 46, "Be still, and know that I am God," threads into my mind. I also think of the fact that Governor Winthrop had a granddaughter named Waitstill. The brain is devious, with altogether too much of a mind of its own. It is good to be still here, to wait on nothing quite so much as the whispers of the Spirit telling me that all shall be well, and all manner of thing shall be well.

It is a day full of hope, unwrapped like a gift before my very eyes. They are wide with wonder. The past recedes like fluid into the distant interstices of memory. Pain is annealed by the cardinal's song. He is not shy. He lifts his head and heaven trembles at the sound. The backyard is made new by five inches of snow. Tulips and daffodils and roses are sleeping their long sleep. I have never seen them prowling around in the night. All is well.

Chapter Eleven

Right, Rights, and Righteousness

WHEN ONE IS WRITING, one usually, or at least should, have some sense of "end" in mind. A culmination, a fulfillment, a goal. And although I was fully aware from my first thoughts about this study that I would eventually examine the virtue of righteousness, I was uncertain of just how to do it. I was at least aware that it should be the culminating study.

We thank Aristotle for introducing us to the philosophical concept of *entelechy*. He understood it as the realization or actualization of potential, that entity toward which all things point. I think it wise to adapt his scheme here, for righteousness appears to be the reality toward which all the "hidden" or lesser-known virtues point. Righteousness, at this point, is the goal of living in God's will, of an especially close relationship between Christian and Christ. The virtues are our stepping-stones. Prolific Bible commentator A. W. Tozer states in *The Root of the Righteous* that "We Please Him most, not by frantically trying to make ourselves good, but by throwing ourselves into His arms with all our imperfections, and believing that he understands everything and loves us still."[1] As Tozer states it, righteousness is an action whereby we throw ourselves on the mercy and care of God. But that kind of self-abandonment seems to negatively impact the word, because righteousness also involves very deliberate ways of living.

It shouldn't be the case, but it seems that there is something just a bit beyond grasp in the word *righteousness*. Some ambiguity unsettles the

1. Tozer, *Root of the Righteous*, 20.

word, as if it somehow lies beyond neat definition. A useful and accurate definition of righteousness might go like this: Seeking the will (or "mind") of Christ in all our actions and services. That is an active definition because righteousness is not like a trophy settled out of reach on a shelf; it is a way of behaving that accords with the revealed will of God and our own conscience.[2]

Yet, righteousness seems a bit difficult to define simply because it is so multistoried in its meanings. *Right* and *rights* are like outlet malls, with one building servicing multiple needs. Before we move further to understand righteousness as a virtue, we have to spend a few moments clarifying the uses of these multilayered terms. The importance of this investigation is that both right and rights can actively work against righteousness if we're not careful.

To enter this network of shaded meanings, consider the simplest meaning first—that is, a right. *Right* is a very old word in the English language, appearing in English forms already in Old English and Middle English and derived from the Latin *rectus*, a military term for a right-handed shield. By the Middle Ages, the word *right* (Old English *riht*) had already taken on many of the complexities that mark the modern English word.[3] The adjective signified the "right" direction, the correct or direct choice. It was also an adverb meaning directly or exactly. It was a noun which meant a privilege or a right, and the compound noun *rightwisnesse* meant righteousness. Suffice it to say that the multiple meanings for one word were getting well established by Middle English (1066–1500).

Having explored several of the meanings of *right* brings us closer to our goal of understanding righteousness. At this point we see it as associated with being correct or living a "straight," unerring life. A second major meaning arises when we think of "rights," those things granted us by a

2. Martin Luther gave extensive and fascinating attention to the kinds of Christian righteousness. "The first is alien righteousness, that is the righteousness of another, instilled from without. This is the righteousness of Christ by which he justifies through faith." Luther adds, "This righteousness is primary; it is the basis, the cause, the source of all our own actual righteousness. For this is the righteousness given in place of the original righteousness lost in Adam." This is primary, but another righteousness follows: "The second kind of righteousness is our proper righteousness, not because we alone work it, but because we work with that first and alien righteousness." This inner righteousness consists of three parts: "a life spent profitably in good works: Love to one's neighbor; meekness and fear toward God." Essentially, the state of righteousness is having the mind of Christ. *Luther's Works, Vol. 31*, II.293–306.

3. The Old English *riht* literally meant straight, and later upright, good, or correct.

government, an agency, or a sovereign. In our country this would consist of the United States Bill of Rights, as drafted by James Madison and as ratified on December 15, 1791, two years after the Constitution went into effect. The famous First Amendment listed five fundamental rights of all citizens: "Congress shall make no law respecting an establishment of religion, or prohibiting the free exercise thereof; or abridging the freedom of speech, or of the press; or the right of the people peaceably to assemble, and to petition the Government for a redress of grievances."[4] Our full Constitution has made us the envy of nations and a model for their own freedoms. But with all freedom lies a danger. What was conceived as a privilege by some, by others is a tool of abuse and self-interest.

For some, freedom to choose becomes an imprisonment in ideology. They can't get beyond the needs of the individual self that freely demands. The issue becomes, what do we do with our rights? As we please? Or as someone else directs? I think of Bob Dylan's lyrics from some years ago: "You're gonna have to serve somebody, yes you are."[5] In a sense Dylan is correct. While we may assert our rights—like the Big Man ghost speaking in C. S. Lewis's *The Great Divorce*: "I'm a plain man that's what I am and I got to have my rights same as anyone else, see?"[6]—even to choose for self is ultimately a choice against God and for the devil.

The rights conferred upon us then, while usually protective and liberating, can also be abused and imprisoning. Insistence upon individual rights, a hallmark of our litigious age, leads to self-satisfaction rather than service for others. I like to watch the news in the evening, before my reading time. The pattern of the evening news is to provide a twelve-minute block of news, then much shorter times to fit the many advertisements. Here in western Michigan those advertisements are often for law firms that promise they will get us our rights and who proudly display the figures they have been awarded. An instant million dollars lies within anyone's

4. When I was growing up, nearly all American history textbooks included an appendix that contained the Constitution and the Bill of Rights and additional amendments. Other important rights in The Bill of Rights include: the right to keep and bear arms (II), the right of the people to be secure in their persons, houses, papers, and effects, the right for freedom from unreasonable searches and seizures (IV), "right to a speedy and public trial" (VI). Afraid that he might have left some necessary rights out, Madison included the ninth, which read: "The enumeration in the Constitution, of certain rights, shall not be construed to deny or disparage others retained by the people."

5. Dylan, "Have to Serve Somebody," *Slow Train Coming* (1979).

6. Lewis, *Great Divorce*, 3.

grasp. All you need to do is get run over by a truck and call someone whose name is also the phone number for the law firm. These firms are relatively obscene in their bold-faced self-aggrandizement.

But so are we who live insisting upon our rights. It is a fraught lifestyle. We just may get our due rights and find that they are hardly what we expected. Contentment is never so much prized as when you don't have it. I might think that I have a right to my beliefs. Yes, that is true. It does not mean that my beliefs are right, or even righteous. In fact, if made just for my self-satisfaction my beliefs may be quite dangerous to my well-being. Righteous beliefs and actions comport with some higher order. But now we are broaching the subject area of righteousness, and we have a bit more work to do before getting there.

Let me summarize the argument thus far. First, we considered the etymology of the word *right* and noted that to be right is to follow a straight, direct path. Moreover, the implication of the word is that one has made a correct choice. Necessarily then, to be right suggests freedom from error or freedom from traveling on bypaths where one might lose the way. That brought us, second, to the matter of rights, those qualities bestowed upon us by our belonging to a group—a nation, a church, Christianity. Implied in *rights* is that we in turn live in service to a society, a congregation, and God. Rights require responsibility.

But we also saw that individual freedom to live according to rights can lead to deleterious effects. Before we move on to righteousness, our third related quality, we should examine that freedom to choose a bit further. The first thing we should bear in mind is that freedom is for or toward something, not for self-gratification. With his customary directness, the prophet Jeremiah makes the point rather nicely: "Therefore, this is what the Lord says: You have not obeyed me; you have not proclaimed freedom for your fellow countrymen. So now I proclaim 'freedom' for you, declares the Lord—'freedom' to fall by the sword, plague and famine. I will make you abhorrent to all the kingdoms of the earth" (34:17). The terrible irony, according to Jeremiah, is how little concerned the people are about their own ignorance. A few chapters earlier Jeremiah questioned:

> Are they ashamed of their loathsome conduct?
> No, they have no shame at all;
> they do not even know how to blush.
> (6:15)

Contentment may at once be the greatest blessing but also the direst curse on a people. Those Jeremiah speaks to have lost any concern for their own sins or the needs of others.

But if Scripture takes to task those individuals who bask in the freedom of self-gratification and who lose awareness of the capacity for wrongdoing ("they do not even know how to blush"), Scripture develops an even more dire warning. It reminds us, repeatedly, that a force of evil, named Satan, is active in the world and trying its best to bend us from the right and our rights. In our God-blessed contentment, our danger is to lose interest in and sight of that one who "prowls around like a roaring lion looking for someone to devour" (1 Pet 5:8). The apostle John wrote of Satan: "He was a murderer from the beginning, not holding to the truth, for there is no truth in him. When he lies, he speaks his native language, for he is a liar and the father of lies" (John 8:44). As N. T. Wright puts it: "Evil is the force of anti-creation, anti-life, the force which opposes and seeks to deface and destroy God's good world of space, time and matter, and above all God's image-bearing human creatures."[7]

Oddly, while prominent in Scripture, Satan has lost credibility in our age. With the tidal swell of pragmatic realism near the turn of the century, Satan became the subject of cartoons and comedy skits. As such he was depicted as a sort of urbane but slightly befuddled gentleman, his topcoat not quite capable of hiding a long red tail and horned feet. In our own age, we don't seem to have time for cosmic disputes. We have businesses to run, payrolls to meet, classes to teach, and hot yoga in the evening. We have dismissed Satan as a progenitor of evil and archenemy of Christendom. Instead, we make "mistakes." George MacDonald, best known for his pioneering fantasy works, also had a practice of writing fully developed but undelivered sermons. One of his strongest is "The Last Farthing," in which he states: "No, there is no escape. There is no heaven with a little hell in it—no plan to retain this or that of the devil in our hearts or our pockets. Out Satan must go, every hair and feather!"[8]

7. Wright, *Evil and the Justice of God*, 89.

8. MacDonald, "Last Farthing." MacDonald elaborates in the next paragraph: "Christ is our righteousness, not that we should escape punishment, still less escape being righteous, but as the live potent creator of righteousness in us, so that we, with our wills receiving his spirit, shall like him resist unto blood, striving against sin; shall know in ourselves, as he knows, what a lovely thing is righteousness, what a mean, ugly, unnatural thing is unrighteousness. He is our righteousness, and that righteousness is no fiction, no pretense, no imputation."

MacDonald recognizes the insidious role of Satan to disrupt Christ's kingdom. Our present age seems uncertain whether Satan even exists, or if it is merely the fabrication of mythology.

That awareness of the work of evil to pervert our freedom and ordained rights, to subvert the right path, and to divorce us from our unity in Christ, leads us now into a consideration of God's righteous kingdom. That kingdom, after all, is what Satan hopes to lead us away from. That kingdom, too, is being shrunken and violated by pragmatic or perverted self-interest. Righteousness, first of all, stands over against some things. Saint Augustine called these things the worldly city. It is an interesting term, for worldliness is insidious, sneaking into our loves and lives, our churches and our Bible studies, our homes and workplaces like a creeping green fog slithering under the doorway and infiltrating our lives. One of the first concepts to suffer under the reign of worldliness is our sense of absolutes.

According to worldly wisdom today, there are no such things as absolutes. Instead, in our deliberately pluralistic society, we have truth according to relativism. The majority view of the society in which we live determines this truth. When a collection of such views coalesce, we have what we call a culture. In turn, our views of what is right or wrong, or what should be right or wrong, are determined by that culture. Never before have pollsters had so much work as they scurry about trying to determine the current truth of affairs. Their work, however, is lessened greatly by the disappearance of the old verities and absolutes. Woe to the person who is found with a copy of the Ten Commandments. Today's culture police might impound them, and perhaps the bearer of them too. We may well have to reassert our rights to believe that such things as the Ten Commandments, or indeed the Bible, hold absolute truths.

Although we rather lightly use *absolute* as an adjective or adverb ("you're absolutely correct"), the concept has a storied past in philosophy stretching back several centuries and typifying God's righteousness. In that instance the word refers to a self-contained truth or value with no need to identify itself according to outside references. Perhaps our earliest experience of it occurs in God's theophany to Moses in Exodus 3:14: "God said to Moses, 'I AM Who I Am.'" Then God adds, "This is my name forever, the name by which I am to be remembered from generation to generation." This is a good example of an absolute, for by so naming himself God establishes that he isn't known by any referent other than himself. Furthermore, that self is all being, and therefore the creator of being for others. Finally, this God is an eternal God always in the state of Being or "I am." He never changes; his word never fails.

We see, then, two strong threats in our time to understanding the righteousness of God. Although receiving far less attention today, which does not mean his power or aims have diminished, Satan works to subvert God and his kingdom. If we take this to mean a lessening interest in divine matters and deteriorating worship of God, clearly this effort is succeeding. In the process, however, certain spiritual ideals are threatened or lost. One such, as we have seen earlier, is a narrowing of human freedom. Furthermore, the sense of absolute truth, embodied in the Holy Trinity, has diminished and been replaced by greater relativity. But there is a third threat to understanding God's righteousness and that is a diminished concern for justice and social service.

The fact is that justice is keenly allied with God's righteousness; indeed, is an integral part of it. R. C. Sproul accurately points out: "When the Bible speaks of justice, it usually links it to divine righteousness. God's justice is according to righteousness. There is no such thing as justice according to unrighteousness. There is no such thing as evil justice in God. The justice of God is always and ever an expression of His holy character."[9] This raises the point about God's justice and God's righteousness that we discussed earlier in this book. Suffice it for our purposes here to add one additional thought, this from John Benton in his influential book *How Can a God of Love Send People to Hell?* Benton observes: "God loves what is right. He will do everything possible to save us, consistent with justice. That is what he has done in Christ. But he will not do anything inconsistent with justice, because there is something even more terrible than sinners going to hell and that is a God who is no longer committed to justice."[10] It may rightly be said that God's righteousness rests upon his justice.

Having considered three contemporary threats to living in righteousness, we are now in a position to examine what that righteousness means for us. In order to keep this discussion manageable, we will consider three main points: first, righteousness as living rightly or correctly, that is, in accord with God's law and expressed will; second, living in justice or with awareness and observance of other people's rights; and third, living a justified life, or one of sanctification, as a consequence of Jesus's righteous sacrifice for us.

9. Sproul, *Holiness of God*, 166.

10. Benton, *How Can a God of Love Send People to Hell?*, 79.

Proverbs could be referred to as the "book of Righteousness" since its authors are intent on examining the blessings and the demands of righteousness upon a believer's life. The series of aphorisms often give a situation with an escape or response, or more frequently bringing antipodes together in tension as with the righteous and the wicked. By creating these tensions, the authors (probably Solomon and his students) hope to shed greater light upon a central theme, such as righteousness. A good example of this type follows: "The Lord's curse is on the house of the wicked, but he blesses the home of the righteous" (Prov 3:33). Compare this to Proverbs 10:2, where we find: "Ill-gotten treasures are of no value, but righteousness delivers from death." In all these righteousness is also associated with wisdom and understanding. As the word is developed later in Proverbs, it is frequently associated with justice (29:7) and honesty (29:27). The New Testament emphasizes the power of righteousness for Christian living; for example, in James 5:16 we find: "The prayer of a righteous man is powerful."

We see as our first point, then, that with the human effort to live rightly, or according to God's will, certain blessings accrue to us and also work to protect us. While Proverbs sets the clash between righteousness and wickedness as a series of tense either/ors, other passages in the Old Testament use the more familiar covenantal pattern of commitments and promises. We see this in a passage like Psalm 37:5-6: "Commit your way to the Lord; trust in him and he will do this: He will make your righteousness shine like the dawn, the justice of your cause like the noonday sun." And that leads us to our second point, that is, living in justice and mindful of other people's intrinsic rights.

A large part of justice in daily living is simply a matter of civility. Over the last decade the denomination of which I am a member has been embroiled in controversy. The subjects vary but a major one of the past few years has to do with sexual orientation and holding office (elder, deacon, or pastor) in the church. As a consequence, a good number of churches have "disaffiliated" from the denomination. At the same time, however, many churches have recognized that it is a human tendency to have strong and opposing feelings, but that God's people can still live in, and rejoice in, loving unity.

Such an issue can be handled civilly, with due respect for others' thoughts and feelings. In fact, that would be a just way of living. Divisiveness and antipathy seldom result in justice. But the example I cite above is only one among dozens that we could find happening every day, all around us. You can make your own list; there's no need to supply mine. What should pierce our thoughts is that justice works two ways: to our fellow humans and environment, and to our God. Job nicely articulated this: "If I have denied justice to my menservants and maidservants when they had a grievance against me, what will I do when God confronts me? What will I answer when called to account? Did not he who made me in the womb make thee? Did not the same one form us both within our mothers?" (Job 31:13–15). Living in justice and righteousness is a matter of individual wholeness and social unity.

As I write this, Percival Everett's book *James* is near the top of *The New York Times* Best Seller list for fiction. The story is narrated by Mark Twain's runaway slave Jim from *Huckleberry Finn.* At times the book is a difficult read, simply because slavery in nineteenth century America was a cruel and callous system. But the book is also penetrating and powerful, especially as Everett probes the depth of character in James as he pursues freedom and justice. At one point his friend Easter observes: "It's a horrible world. White people try to tell us that everything will be just fine when we go to heaven. My question is, Will they be there? If so, I might make other arrangements."[11] We can easily understand Easter's point when we understand that justice is the daily effort to translate heavenly righteousness into our earthly affairs.

In their book *Sin, Death, and the Devil,* Robert Jenson and Carl Braaten point out that "History's whole dismal armory of sins, so impressive from a distance, is only a selection of ways not to be one thing, righteous. We are created to be righteous, that is, to form one community with each other and with the persons of the triune God, in which each of us takes her or his unique place and uses that place as an opportunity to love the rest of us. Any sin humanity can think of is simply one or another way of refusing to do this."[12] In their shalom argument, Jenson and Braaten tend to see righteousness as a divine circularity, flowing from God to humans and back to God. Something of that also comes to bear as we turn to our third point—righteousness and justification.

Several times in this book I have sung the praises of justice. Rightfully so, since justice is knit closely with righteousness and most other virtues. In fact, by this point we might say that without justice there is no righteousness. But there is another sense in which justice presents

11. Everett, *James,* 151.

12. Jenson and Braaten, *Sin, Death, and the Devil,* 2.

problematic issues. Were Jesus to judge me according to my own virtues and righteousness, I would stand guilty in the dock. On the other hand, with the allied word *justification* (according to Jesus's own righteousness) I stand welcomed into the heavenly kingdom. With Jesus's righteousness imposed upon me in such a way that my injustice and guilt are nowhere to be seen I will be totally righteous for the first time. Righteousness in this sense seems to be something we are growing toward. Our acts of justice and our moral lives of righteousness are shadowy stages we grow through on our way to fulfillment in Christ. In the heavenly kingdom, there cannot be injustice, nor can there be anything like unrighteousness. We will have learned the nature of truth perfectly. We will be justified.

Thus far in this chapter I have provided biblical citations primarily from the Old Testament. I did so to show two things. First, the concept of righteousness is thoroughly ingrained in the daily life and religion of the Hebrew nation. Second, the whole of the Old Testament is a looking forward to the fulfilment, the goal, the *entelechy* of righteousness in Christ. Upon that goal rests our justification.

So too the Old Testament has a profoundly futuristic bent. In this way many of the references to righteousness also look ahead to Jesus's incarnation as the righteous one. For example, Jeremiah 29:11–12 has these well-known lines: "'For I know the plans I have for you,' declares the Lord, 'plans to prosper you and not to harm you, plans to give you hope and a future. Then you will call upon me and come and pray to me, and I will listen to you. You will seek me and find me when you seek me with all your heart." In his messianic prophecy, Isaiah states: "Of the increase of his government and peace there will be no end. He will reign on David's throne and over his kingdom, establishing and upholding it with justice and righteousness from that time on and forever" (Isa 9:7).

Now we are at the point probably where we are asking, what exactly is justification? Justification is the act whereby humans are made righteous by the sacrifice of Jesus.[13] The act of the crucifixion, in spiritual terms, is the process by which Jesus took upon himself the full penalty of our sins and bestowed upon us in its place his own righteousness. By justification, Jesus sees us as forgiven, holy, and righteous, just as if we had never sinned. Romans 4:23–25 makes it explicit: "The words 'it was

13. In the third book of *The Institutes* John Calvin has a great deal to say about justification: "Therefore, we explain justification simply as the acceptance with which God receives us into his favor as righteous men. And we say that it consists in the remission of sins and the imputation of Christ's righteousness" (III.xi.2).

credited to him' were written not for him alone, but also for us, to whom God will credit righteousness—for us who believe in him who raised Jesus our Lord from the dead. He was delivered over to death for our sins and was raised to life for our justification."

That is not only a nexus between the Old and New Testaments, it is the true *entelechy* of all our searching and striving. It is home after the hard journey, peace after the long battle. All that we have deeply yearned for, with that longing that begins in the soul's secret places, is fulfilled in the righteousness and forgiveness of the Lamb.

Chapter Twelve

Virtuous Souls

We humans tend to think of virtues in the abstract.

The vices are readily apparent. They constitute the evening news and saturate print media. They are inescapable. They storm into our church life, our professional life, and our home life with all the stealth of a rogue elephant. Everyone notices; everyone talks about it.

But virtue? Not so much. It is not a case where the virtues are difficult to talk about, or as if they are complicated issues best left for philosophers, ethics classes, and ministerial retreats. They just seem to have dropped from our daily vocabulary, while the vices enjoy an undue proportion.

It seems, furthermore, that nearly anyone can name most, if not all, of the traditional vices, perhaps stumbling over wrath or gluttony—those mysterious and fuzzy vices that nonetheless are known by anyone that experiences them. Beyond the so-called "divine triad" of faith, hope, and love, however, people are hard-pressed to name additional virtues. People frequently mix in a few of the fruits of the Spirit, but these are even harder to remember.

In contemporary usage, so many virtues are issued forth that one turns away defeated before even attempting to fulfill them in life. Besides the "divine triad," traditional virtues include four—prudence, temperance, fortitude, and justice—for a total of seven. But humanity is ceaselessly clever in inventing ways to be good, even if it is not particularly adept in practicing them. If one did a haphazard search on Google, for example, the search engine will turn up questions related to your inquiry. For example, my search raised the question: "What are the Top 52 Virtues?" The question returned such answers as "assertiveness," and "forgiveness." I would imagine that if one is assertive, which seems a very odd virtue to me, one also has to be forgiven quite often. In additional lists such terms as honesty, chastity, kindness, and humility appear. They are endless. Someone might decide that it's a whole lot easier to have vices than virtues.

The study of virtues sometimes seems to boil down to the simple idea that we humans are not as bad as everybody keeps telling us. You can do the math: if you have thirty-seven of the fifty-two virtues and only two of the seven major vices, you are living a pretty good life. Sometimes we designate virtues in the same way that Supreme Court Justice Potter Stewart defined pornography: "I know it when I see it."

But it's all so soft and easy. It's like trying to lose weight by watching weight-loss commercials all day. As I understand them, virtues are something to work for. They are hard won. Humility takes a concerted effort, exercised in the furious swirl of daily living. Exercise it enough—countless times—and it just might become a habit, a way of life. One grows into a virtuous soul, that moment when virtue is not just something we seek but indeed is now part of our very nature. Then we cannot help acting virtuously.

To achieve that state, that nature of being, we are helped along the way by others who point a way we should go. More than all the printed words, more than all the exhortations and sermons, a mentor who exemplifies the virtues is our surest guide. Indeed, some of our mentors have feet of clay. No one attains perfection in this life, certainly not on their own capability. But if we work hard, we can see through their human fallenness and fallibility to a virtuous soul. Sometimes we conclude the search with dismay; there only seems to be a vapor within. I am still puzzling over Charles Dunlap McNeese III.

I have written occasionally about writing in this book, mentioning some of the steps or practices. One of my steps, as I mentioned, is to engage in interviews. This is for two reasons: to test my ideas with and against others, and to see what ideas others bring to the table. In the process of writing about virtues, I happened to consider interviewing Charles. I thought a contemporary seminarian might be able to shed some light. Be that as it may, the interview might have gone like this.

*****

He sat across from me, blinking like an owl through rimless spectacles perched halfway down his nose. He wore a sport coat that I would have bet, were I a betting man, came from the Salvation Army Thrift Shop. Nothing wrong with that, except it billowed around him like a gunny sack and barely hid his dirty T-shirt. For a moment I thought I was back in the 1960s. His name, I had learned through a quick online check, was Charles Dunlop McNeese III. He had hinted when I called that he was a marginal member of some tire fortune. "You can call me Charles," he informed me now with a limp handshake.

He was a senior at Blythedale Theological Seminary, and part of the bribery to get him to talk with me was lunch at Rose's Diner, which despite its mundane name was one of the more expensive lunch stops in town. His hamburger and fries set me back $29.95, the milkshake another $11.95. He better be worth it. I had a cup of gazpacho and water. And a killer view of Blythedale Lake through the picture window.

I tried to break the ice as he gobbled at that hamburger like a famished turkey.

"And how are things at Happy Valley?" I asked.

He paused, staring at me with a mouth full of hamburger. "Happy Valley?" he asked. As if it were a remote planet.

"Blythedale," I said. "It comes from the Old English words for 'happy region', or 'happy valley.'"

He commenced chewing again. "I didn't know that," he muttered.

"Well, of course. You've probably been too busy studying Greek and Hebrew at the seminary."

"Ah, actually we don't study those languages anymore. There are plenty of good translations of the Bible and you can look up anything you want on the computer." He set his hamburger down, swirled a French fry in ketchup and sucked it off.

"Interesting. I suppose that gives you more time to study the Bible?"

"Not exactly. Although we did have two mandatory courses in non-canonical books. You know, the Apocrypha?"

"I see." I stirred my gazpacho. For fifteen bucks, it wasn't too bad. Charles finished his meat and started popping ketchup-soaked fries in his mouth. "An interesting fact," I observed, "Jesus quoted the Old Testament dozens of times."

Charles nodded.

"Jesus never once quoted from a single apocryphal book."

"So?"

"Just an observation. Why don't you tell me a little bit about the courses you have taken?"

His plate empty, Charles Dunlop McNeese III slurped deeply of vanilla milkshake and peered at me over his glasses, still propped low on his nose. "Well, I'm midway through a three-quarter-long course called Biblical Feminism." He drew circles on the damp table with his forefinger. "It divides into three parts: Women in the Bible, Women in culture, Women in the church. Sort of a combination of hermeneutics and social history. You know, women are hot right now."

"Sounds interesting," I said. "What else?"

"Mind if I smoke a cigar?"

"This is a no-smoking restaurant, Charles. In fact, all restaurants are."

"A shame, that. We've lost our decency."

"Yes, well. Try to hold off. Patience is a virtue, you know."

"Never trust a man without a vice, is what I say."

"Just about everyone's got a vice, Charles. It's this thing about fallen nature."

"Don't tell me you believe in that old saw. Humankind is pretty good. On its way to becoming perfect."

"It just needs a little more engineering, right?"

Charles nodded vigorously as he slurped up the last of the milkshake through a straw. "Humanity. Human justice. That's where it's at, man."

"What? I'm confused. What is where it's at?"

"Social justice. Just think—what percentage of humans are marginalized? 75, 80 percent, I've heard some people say."

"But, Charles. If 80 percent were marginalized they would be the majority. They couldn't be marginalized."

"Maybe I mean needy. We have to preach the social gospel for the needy."

"Please don't get me wrong here. By the way, could you use another milkshake?"

"I'm good. Maybe coffee in a minute or two."

"Okay. What I was going to ask is this. Do you do things to help the needy? I mean, are you active now? Or is this something for you to preach about later?"

"I'm not really sure I'm cut out to be a preacher, you know? I would like to run a nonprofit or something. Maybe a program."

"Admirable. Meanwhile, why don't you tell me what else you've studied? There has to be more than your courses on women and the Apocrypha."

"My first year I had a wonderful yearlong course in mythology. You know, we studied deities from all around the world. Hinduism. Buddhism. Islam. Confucianism."

"Sounds like World Religions."

"Sort of. But this was about the myths, the stories people told themselves to give their life meaning." Charles began expounding about myths and mythology. I finished my soup. He lost me somewhere with a remote Tibetan tribe and its nature goddess. A bit rudely, perhaps, I interrupted him.

"Charles, please tell me. Do you study any creeds? Any doctrines?"

"Why? They're old. People aren't interested in them today."

"How about theology?"

"Oh, sure. We have a circle group every Monday where we drink coffee and share our thoughts about God."

"Actually, I was hoping you could help me with a project. But I think we'll let it go."

"No. Please. Tell me. I'd be happy to help in any way I can."

"Well, I was wondering if maybe you could tell me what grace is."

"Oh, that's easy. It's people being nice to each other."

"You mean like gracious?"

"Exactly."

"But not divine grace?"

"Oh, I see. You're trying to trick me. I know better. Divine grace is an outmoded concept. It's like wearing a raincoat on a sunny day."

"We don't need it anymore?"

"Right. I told you humanity is essentially good."

"I'm almost afraid to ask . . . but do you believe in sin?"

"Well. It's possible. Mostly there are just things people do. They need the freedom to do what they want."

"As long as it doesn't intrude on another's freedom. How about Satan? What are your thoughts?"

Charles smiled broadly. I thought, with a shiver of dread, he's actually enjoying himself. It's a wonderful world of unbelief. All God's children got shoes and they're just dancing through the daisies. At last he broke out in a deep chuckle.

"I think I'm catching on to your game," Charles said. He actually wagged his finger at me. As if he had caught me swiping cookies from the cookie jar. "Of course there's a Satan. Who do you think starts all these wars? Ukraine? Lebanon? Gaza? We call that the work of Satan, right?"

"Okay. So he's . . .or is it she? So Satan is pretty powerful and she gets good people to do some bad things?"

"I would say that pretty much sums it up. Every person has a right to be safe, to be comfortable, to do freely what they want to do insofar as they don't impinge on someone else's freedom. When they do, it's a bad thing. Satan is just a name for doing that bad thing, for hurting someone else's freedom or impinging upon their free choice."

"Well, Charles. This just gets more interesting as it goes along. May I just push it a little bit further? If I understand you right, there isn't anything like a bad person; there's just persons who might do a bad thing."

"Right. And those people who do a bad thing can't help it."

"I assume they act badly because of their formative environment. That is, they grew up in a society that mistreated them, so they don't know the difference. They think their upbringing is the only way to be, and so will mistreat others."

"Exactly. I'm glad you agree."

"Please, Charles. I don't know if I agree or not. I'm just gathering information on how a contemporary seminarian might think about these issues. I'm a writer, see? That's how I write. I gather research."

"I don't see how that can work. You mean, who you take for lunch determines what you write?"

"No, Charles. That is not it at all. Not at all. First, I interview many people from many paths in life. Second, I research a ton of books, magazines, and such. Then I do have some ideas of my own. I'm not a robot."

"But still. That's the key issue. Not everyone thinks as you do. Some call your wrong their right. Let me give you an example. But first, I would really like some coffee. And maybe a piece of pie. Apple. A la mode."

"Well, of course." I waved Sophia over. She took her time, angling through some squares of evening light spread out upon the floor. I would move slow too if I had to wear those tight black leggings. Must take a half hour to get those things on and off. She dug her order book out of her white apron on the way over. I ordered for myself too. I thought I would need the energy to get through Charles's example. In my mind's eye, which has always suffered from presbyopia, I tried to see Charles as a fifty-year-old minister somewhere. Couldn't see out quite that far.

Charles appeared to be floating into a nap, waiting for dessert to come. I stared out the window over the lake. A flotilla of small sailboats skipped the light fandango before the wind. It was a pretty day, a nice lake. Ducks slid to a halt in the shallows. It must have been good fishing because they all went tail up in unison. Probably telling dirty jokes in hiding.

For some reason I wanted to smoke a pipe. Maybe it was Charles's reference to a cigar.

I used to smoke a pipe. I wish I still did. I tried cigarettes once, a pack of Pall Malls, but didn't much care for them. It has been about ten years since I quit altogether. But I still miss it. Nothing fancy. I smoked about three different corn cob pipes, rotating them throughout the day. There's no better smoke once you break in one of those cobs. I ordered my tobacco from a shop in New York City; got it cheap. And it was top-flight tobacco, smooth and tasty, with a sailboat on the pouch. Ah, there's the connection. The old subconscious is alive and well. The sailboats blurred on the other side of the lake.

Charles's head leaned forward, a trickle of drool etched down his chin. Pie and coffee were in front of each of us. This lunch was going to cost me. Might as well get my money's worth, although I didn't think I would be mining for deep pockets of ore in Charles.

I barked his name. His eyes fluttered. He just about had his nose in the coffee.

"It's getting late, Charles. We're the only people left in here from lunch."

"Whassat?"

"Let's finish up. I still have a few more questions."

"Fire away." He slurped his coffee.

"But, first," I said, "you were going to give me an example."

"I don't . . . I'm a little sleepy. I'm not sure what I was going to say."

"I understand—"

"Oh! It was from my mythology class. About the Lakota Sioux, plains Indians."

"Okay."

"When they went into war, it was a big thing to kill the enemy. With a knife, bow and arrow or however. But the biggest thing was to 'count coup,' to ride into battle on your pony and get close enough to the enemy to touch him. That was the biggest deal."

"Okay. The point is?"

"Just that not everyone acts as expected. Not everyone honors the same things."

"Interesting. Do you think there are any universals?"

"Probably not in the sense you're thinking of. Like I said, what you may think wrong another person in another culture might think right."

"So it's all relative? How about pride? Is it always wrong to be proud?

"I suppose," Charles said, "it depends on how we define *pride*. If one of my friends does something really outstanding, I can say, 'I'm really proud of you.' That would be a compliment. Nothing wrong with that."

"Certainly. But by *pride* we traditionally mean an excessive emphasis upon one's own ability and worth. A sense that I am superior to all those around me. At its extreme end, pride demeans and belittles other people as inferior. At this point pride makes one believe that he or she doesn't need any others—and certainly not God."

"Well, that's pretty strongly put. Still, I would say it is natural for certain gifted leaders, an Einstein say, or a king or ruler, to feel that they are important and self-sufficient."

"So once again it's relative to the situation one finds oneself in?"

"Would you want a president who had to consult with everyone before he or she acted, who didn't dare make up their own mind without talking it over?"

"Yes. I have to admit that is very much the kind of president I would like to have. One who consults with others instead of playing Lone Ranger. And even the Lone Ranger had Tonto."

"That's because you have been shaped by your environment that way." Charles held my glance, a forkful of pie halfway to his mouth.

"I must say that I believe I have a little more individuality and personhood than you give me credit for. I mean, I'm not a pet dog who has been conditioned one way. Remember when God said to Jeremiah: 'Before I formed you in the womb I knew you, before you were born I set you apart; I appointed you as a prophet to the nations?'"

"You read Jeremiah! I mean that is *really* ancient history. I don't know if any of my friends read the Old Testament anymore."

"But some truths are eternal. Not everything is relative to the age. For example, when did 'There is a God' cease to be true?'"

"I'm not sure there's still a *need* for a God. Things wear out, grow outmoded. If someone feels guilty now, they just take some weed."

"Charles, we're not getting very far with that universal. I meant it as a joke. Let's try one of those vices that everyone seems to feel guilty about. Let's try the other end of the spectrum—lust."

"Oh, really. You're not going to waste time on that old saw. Talk about ancient history."

"Actually, the concern is ancient. When he totaled up the vices, Aristotle began with lust at the bottom, the lowest step on the ladder of sins. Lust, he said, the vestige of the animal kingdom in us. In the body it is situated from the waist down—no higher. But Aristotle also argued that we are not animals but willful beings of rational capabilities. Thus, the animal vestige dishonors us and must be controlled."

"Whoa, Nelly. You really get carried away with lust. You better slow down and eat some pie. Cool down, you know."

"I'm not carried away, Charles. I'm just trying to understand some old beliefs through modern eyes."

"Simple enough. Almost all the vices and the virtues too, both of them, are daydreams of fearmongers in the past."

"Now it's my turn: Whoa, Nelly yourself. You can't mean that."

"Sure. We can't afford to be like those people going around with heads bowed and shoulders slumped under the weight of imagined sins. There's too much to live for. Besides, your terms are all old-fashioned too."

"I am a good bit older than you. I suppose it's natural that my language isn't up to date."

"For example, I haven't heard anyone use the term *lust* since I was wee high."

"So what's the substitute?"

"Just *sex.* It's not as animal-like as lust."

"Granted. But it's a totally different animal too. Lust carries the meaning of uncontrolled passion. In fact, all the vices—lust, pride, sloth, greed, envy, wrath, and gluttony—are marked by their excessive nature, how they can become obsessive in a person."

"Well, I'm not sure," Charles mused. He picked up the crust of his pie with a thumb and forefinger, swirled it in a puddle of ice cream, and popped it in his mouth. As he munched on it, he said, "I don't think I do any of those things. Do you?"

"Are you proud of not doing them?"

"Ha. I see your trap. Nope. I'm not proud either. I get by. I go with the flow."

"Take one of your examples. Can we say that when one's use of sex is aberrant or excessive, then it becomes the vice of lust?"

"I suppose. That's why I practice moderation in all things."

"But you have a healthy appetite."

"I do enjoy good food. That's not a sin."

"Perhaps. But can you agree with me that the notorious seven vices are root sins. Out of their swamp waters, breed countless other sins that plague humankind. Think of it like COVID-19, which has since bred many similar but different viruses. All of them, however, share fundamental similarities to the original COVID-19. So too greed might breed stinginess, and a proud spirit might breed scorn."

"I think I see your point," Charles said.

"But we also have to see that each root vice obviates the opposing virtue. For example, if you are obsessed by lust, or sex in your case, it's pretty hard to practice chastity, right."

"True. But why is it so much easier to practice a vice than the virtue?"

"That, Charles, is the million-dollar question. Most answer it by pointing out that the very first sin was pride. Turning to our way over God's way."

"You mean in Eden?"

"Some scholars place it even earlier. When Lucifer was thrown out of heaven because he wanted to be like God. But yes, in Eden too. Before Eve or Adam ever took the fruit, they committed the sin of pride—wanting to be like God. Satan didn't have much trouble tempting them. He knew firsthand from experience just what would work."

Charles leaned back from a table full of empty plates. "Well," he said. "I guess I have something to think about. But I think right now I really need a nap. This was good food here. Maybe we could do this again. I know some other really neat places to eat."

On the way out, Charles asked if I could give him a ride home. I pointed out that the seminary housing was only three blocks away.

"I know," he said. "But that's pretty far to walk on a full stomach."

When I dropped him off, Charles called out, "Until next time!"

Bibliography

Alter, Robert. *The Wisdom Books*. New York: W. W. Norton, 2010.

Aquinas, Thomas. *An Aquinas Reader.* Edited by Mary T. Clark. Garden City, NY: Doubleday Image, 1972.

Augustine, Saint. *City of God*. Garden City, NY: Doubleday Image, 1958.

Beck, Martha. *The Way of Integrity*. New York: Penguin, 2022.

Benton, John. *How Can a God of Love Send People to Hell?* Hartfordshire, UK: Evangelical, 1985.

Bonhoeffer, Dietrich. *The Cost of Discipleship*. New York: Simon & Schuster, 1995.

Bussie, Jacqueline A. *Love Without Limits*. Minneapolis: Broadleaf, 2022.

Calvin, John. *A Compend of The Institutes of the Christian Religion*. Edited by Hugh T. Kerr. Philadelphia: Westminster John Knox, 1976.

———. *The Institutes of the Christian Religion*. Edited by John T. McNeill. Louisville: Westminster John Knox, 1960.

Carney, Glandion, and William Long. *Trusting God Again*. Downers Grove, IL: InterVarsity, 1995.

Chapman, Chuck. *Finding Your Way Without Losing Yourself: The Path of Integrity*. N.P.: Praus Media, 2024.

Chaucer, Geoffrey. "Prologue." In *The Canterbury Tales, Chaucer's Major Poetry*, edited by Albert C. Baugh, 217–55. New York: Appleton-Century-Crofts, 1963.

Coleridge, Samuel Taylor. "To a Young Ass." In *Samuel Taylor Coleridge: The Complete Poems,* edited by William Keach, 66. London: Penguin Classics, 1997.

cummings, e. e. "I Thank You God." In *100 Selected Poems*, 75–77. New York: Grove, 1978.

Cussler, Clive. *The Sacred Stone*. New York: G. P. Putnam's, 2008.

Dante, Alighieri. *The Divine Comedy*. Translated by Dorothy Sayers and Barbara Reynolds. Middlesex, UK: Penguin, 1977.

De Young, Kevin. *The Good News We Almost Forgot*. Chicago: Moody, 2010.

DeYoung, Rebecca Konyndyk. *Glittering Vices*. 2nd ed. Grand Rapids: Brazos, 2020.

Dickinson, Emily. *Final Harvest: Emily Dickinson's Poems*. Edited by Thomas H. Johnson. Boston: Little, Brown, 1961.

Eliot, T. S. "The Waste Land." In *Collected Poems 1909–1962*, 51–76. New York: Harcourt, Brace and Company, 1997.

Emerson, Ralph Waldo. "Nature." In *The American Tradition in Literature*, 12th ed., Volume 1, edited by George Perkins and Barbara Perkins, 1282–1309. New York: McGraw-Hill, 2009.

———. "Self-Reliance." In *The American Tradition in Literature*, 12th ed., Volume 1, edited by George Perkins and Barbara Perkins, 1304–50. New York: McGraw-Hill, 2009.

Estes, Daniel J. *The Message of Wisdom: Learning and Living the Way of the Lord*. Downers Grove, IL: InterVarsity, 2020.

Everett, Percival. *James*. New York: Doubleday, 2024.

Foster, Richard. *Life with God*. New York: Harper One, 2005.

———. *Streams of Living Water*. San Francisco: HarperSanFrancisco, 1998.

Franklin, Benjamin. *The Autobiography*. In *The American Tradition in Literature*, vol. 1, 12th ed., edited by George Perkins and Barbara Perkins, 285–316. New York: McGraw-Hill, 2009.

———. *Poor Richard's Almanack*. Edited by Paul A. Volker. New York: Skyhorse, 2007.

Goethe, Johann Wolfgang von. *Wilhelm Meister's Apprenticeship*. Edited by Eric Blackall. Princeton: Princeton University Press, 1995.

Golden, Kate. *The Sacred Stones Trilogy*. New York: Penguin Random House, 2022.

Hoezee, Scott. *The Riddle of Grace*. Grand Rapids: Eerdmans, 1996.

Hopkins, Gerard Manley. "God's Grandeur." In *Gerard Manley Hopkins*, edited by Catherine Phillips, 128. Oxford: Oxford University Press, 1986.

Hume, David. "On Miracles." In *An Enquiry Concerning Human Understanding*, 79–95. New York: Oxford University Press, 1986.

Jenson, Robert W., and Carl E. Braaten. *Sin, Death, and the Devil*. Grand Rapids: Eerdmans, 2000.

Keller, Timothy. *Counterfeit Gods*. New York: Riverhead, 2009.

———. *The Reason for God*. New York: Riverhead/Penguin, 2009.

Kierkegaard, Søren. *Fear and Trembling*. Translated by Alistair Hannay. New York: Penguin, 1985.

———. *The Present Age*. Translated by Alexander Dru. New York: Harper Torchbooks, 1962.

Lamott, Anne. *Traveling Mercies: Some Thoughts on Faith*. New York: Pantheon, 1999.

Lewis, C. S. *The Abolition of Man*. New York: Macmillan, 1975.

———. *The Four Loves*. New York: HarperOne, 2017.

———. *The Great Divorce*. New York: HarperCollins, 1973.

———. *Mere Christianity*. New York: Simon & Schuster Touchstone, 1996.

———. *Till We Have Faces*. Grand Rapids: Eerdmans, 1979.

———. *The Weight of Glory*. Grand Rapids: Eerdmans, 1973.

Lockyer, Herbert. *The 7 Pillars of Wisdom*. New Kensington, PA: Whitaker, 2013.

Lucado, Max. *Grace: More Than We Deserve, Greater Than We Imagine*. Nashville: Thomas Nelson, 2012.

Luther, Martin. *Luther's Works. Volume 31: Career of the Reformer 1*. Edited by Jaroslav Pelikan et al. Philadelphia: Fortress, 1999.

———. *Luther's Works. Vol. 35: Word and Sacrament I*. Edited by Jaroslav Pelikan et al. Philadelphia: Fortress, 1999.

———. "A Mighty Fortress." *Psalter Hymnal*. Grand Rapids: The Christian Reformed Church, 1959.

MacDonald, George. "The Last Farthing." https://www.mercyonall.org/posts/the-last-farthing.

Mikalatos, Matt, and Kathy Kang. *Loving Disagreement: Fighting for Community through the Fruit of the Spirit.* Colorado Springs: NavPress, 2023.

Miller, J. Hillis. *The Disappearance of God.* New York: Schocken, 1965.

Miller, Paul E. *Love Walked Among Us.* Colorado Springs: NavPress, 2014.

Milton, John. *Paradise Lost, The Complete Poetical Works of John Milton.* Edited by Douglas Bush. Boston: Houghton Mifflin, 1965.

Nietzsche, Friedrich. *Thus Spoke Zarathustra.* Translated by Walter Kaufmann. New York: Viking, 1971.

Packer, J. I. *Knowing God.* Downers Grove, IL: InterVarsity, 1976.

Phillips, Richard D. *What's So Great About the Doctrine of Grace*? Sanford, FL: Ligionier Ministries, 2018.

Plantinga, Cornelius, Jr. *Beyond Doubt: A Devotional Response to Questions of Faith.* Grand Rapids: Bible Way, 1986.

Sayers, Dorothy L. "Introduction" to *The Divine Comedy: Purgatory,* 9–72. Middlesex, England: Penguin, 1977.

Shakespeare, William. *King Richard the Third.* In *The Oxford Shakespeare: The Complete Plays,* edited by Stanley Wells et al., 183–222. Oxford: Oxford University Press, 2005.

———. *The Merchant of Venice.* In *The Oxford Shakespeare: The Complete Plays,* edited by Stanley Wells et al., 453–88. Oxford: Oxford University Press, 2005.

Smedes, Lewis. *Mere Morality.* Grand Rapids: Eerdmans, 1983.

Solzhenitsyn, Aleksandr. "The Templeton Address." In *In the World: Reading and Writing as a Christian*, edited by John H. Timmerman and Donald R. Hettinga, 385–97. Grand Rapids: Baker, 1987.

Sproul, R. C. *The Holiness of God.* Wheaton, IL: Tyndale, 1993.

Stob, Henry. *Ethical Reflections: Essays on Moral Themes.* Grand Rapids: Eerdmans, 1978.

Stott, John. *The Cross of Christ.* Downers Grove, IL: InterVarsity, 1986.

———. *Romans: God's Good News for the World.* Downers Grove, IL: InterVarsity, 1999.

Tozer, A. W. *The Root of the Righteous.* Chicago: Moody, 2015.

Willard, Dallas. *The Allure of Gentleness.* New York: HarperOne, 2015.

Wolterstorff, Nicholas. *Journey Toward Justice: Personal Encounters in the Global South.* Grand Rapids: Baker Academic, 2013.

———. *Justice in Love.* Grand Rapids: Eerdmans, 2015.

———. *Justice: Rights and Wrongs.* Princeton: Princeton University Press, 2010.

———. *Until Justice and Peace Embrace.* Grand Rapids: Eerdmans, 1987.

Wordsworth, William. "The Tables Turned." In *Anthology of Romanticism*, edited by Ernest Bernbaum, 130. New York: The Ronald Press, 1948.

Wright, N. T. *Evil and the Justice of God.* Downers Grove, IL: InterVarsity, 2006.

Yancey, Philip. *What's So Amazing About Grace?* Grand Rapids: Zondervan, 1997.

General Index

Scripture Index

SCRIPTURE INDEX

www.ingramcontent.com/pod-product-compliance
Lightning Source LLC
LaVergne TN
LVHW090521110826
845146LV00003B/942

* 9 7 9 8 3 8 5 2 4 9 1 7 6 *